WAR DIARY
―――OF THE―――
1st LIFE GUARDS

*FIRST YEAR,
1914—1915.*

Lt.-Col. H.H. The Duke of Teck.
Commanding 1st Life Guards
October 5th–19th

Lt.-Col. E.H. Brassey M.V.O.
Commanding 1st Life Guards.
October 19th–November 1st

Lt.-Col. E.B. Cook, M.V.O.
Commanding Composite Regiment.
August 15th – October 22nd 1914.

Lt.-Col. Sir George Holford.
K.C.V.O. C.I.E.
Commanding Reserve Regiment
1st Life Guards.

Lt.-Col. The Hon. A.F. Stanley.
D.S.O.
Commanding 1st Life Guards
From November 1st 1914 to date.

1st LIFE GUARDS.

Date of Composite Regiment leaving England .. 15th August, 1914.

Date of Regiment leaving for Ludgershall .. .. 2nd September, 1914.

,, ,, ,, ,, Belgium .. .. .. 4th October, 1914.

Divisional Squadron left England .. .. .. 4th August, 1915

Number of N.C.O.'s and Men who have left England to join Expeditionary Force since beginning of War:—

1st Life Guards .. .. 696 ⎫
Dragoons, etc. .. .. 543 ⎬ Total 1,239.

Officer Commanding Composite Regiment: Colonel E. B. COOK, M.V.O.

Officers Commanding Regiment:—

Lieut.-Colonel H.H. DUKE OF TECK, G.C.B., G.C.V.O., C.M.G.
,, E. H. BRASSEY, M.V.O.
,, HON. A. F. STANLEY, D.S.O.

N.C.O.'S AND MEN.

	Killed.	Died of Wounds, etc.	Wounded.	Missing.	Prisoners of War.
1st Life Guards ..	34	14	96	17	15
Dragoons	40	—	129	60	14
Total	74	14	225	77	29

MAP SHOWING THE PROGRESS OF THE COMPOSITE REGIMENT

Prepared from one lent by Major Genl. the Hon. C. Bingham, C.B.

0 10 20 30 English Miles
0 10 20 30 40 50 Kilomètres

London: Witherby & Co.

Stanford's Geog! Estabt, London.

Extracts from the Private Diary of
Lieutenant-Colonel E. B. COOK, M.V.O.,
Composite Regiment, Household Cavalry.

Aug. 14.—Orders for Composite Regiment to leave to-morrow for Foreign Service. Interview with King and Queen. Lodged Standards Buckingham Palace.

Aug. 15.—Left Hyde Park Barracks 9.40 A.M., 1st Life Guards' Squadron 11.20, Royal Horse Guards' Squadron 2.30, 2nd Life Guards' Squadron (from Windsor) 2.30, all for Southampton en route for HAVRE. S.S. "Thespis" started embarking at 8 P.M., got finished at 5 A.M. Bad arrangements for shipping wagons. Horses were all on by 2 A.M.

Aug. 16.—Left SOUTHAMPTON at 5.30 A.M., arrived off HAVRE at 3.30 P.M. Got a great reception entering dock. Disembarked very well. Went into rest camp 5 miles out. Got there at midnight. Astor's horse fell coming, hurt A's leg.

Aug. 17.—Rest camp. Got orders to leave by train to——. Left camp.

Aug. 18.—Left H. by train 9.45 A.M. Arrived HAUTMONT 2.30 A.M., via AMIENS—BUSIGNY.

Aug. 19.—Detrained HAUTMONT 2.30 A.M. Marched to Dimont. Billeted. Brigade Headquarters here. (1) C.B. at MARPENT-JEUMONT. (2) C.B. DAMOUSIES-OBRECHES-DIMECHAUX. (3) C.B. COUSOLRE-COLLENET. (4) C.B. DIMONT—LEZ FONTAINES—WATTIGUES. C.D. Headquarters AIBES.

Aug. 20.—Rest DIMONT. First rest last night. Had bath and change. Bed 9 P.M. Slept till 7.30. Very comfortable billet and good bed.

Aug. 21.—Left at 5.30 A.M., marched through AIBES. Crossed frontiers into BELGIUM at JEUMONT. Got in touch with German patrols. Billeted HARVENG at 8 P.M. Very crowded.

Aug. 22.—Left billets at 11 A.M., heard guns to our right. Went to support 2nd and 3rd Brigades at HALTE. Stayed there till 7 P.M. Artillery came into action at 5 P.M. Left for BAISAIRE. Arrived midnight. 1 horse shot. 16th Lancers killed several Uhlans. 1 officer Greys wounded. Firing all evening on canal line.

Aug 23.—BAISAIRE. Left billets at 5.40 P.M., moved to SAULTAIN. BETHELL's troop took German officers prisoners and reported many Germans killed on canal line. Heard firing all evening. Returned to SAULTAIN and dug trenches. Slept in street.

Aug. 24.—Retired at dawn to FT. LE CROISE then took up position till 3 P.M., when we were ordered to entrench SAULTAIN. 6th Dragoon Guards at CURGIES. 3rd Hussars just beyond.

Aug. 25.—German Infantry attacks SAULTAIN. We evacuate. Had to leave our entrenching tools and some maps. Got shelled a good deal. Had a hot time of it in evening. Got into VIESTRY 11 P.M., could not stop there, went to BEAUMONT, 12.30 A.M.

Aug. 26.—Went to LIGNEY and fought Battle of Cambrai. I was sent to support General SNOW. Was under shell fire. Did rearguard to General SNOW's division all night. Very trying time. No sleep.

Aug. 27.—PERONNE. Nasty rearguard action at VENDHUILE. I in command of the rearguard of ourselves, 6 troops 3rd Hussars, and the Regiment of 6th Dragoon Guards; badly shelled coming. Retiring on LEMPIRE. 6th Dragoon Guards lost 6 officers—retired by night to HAM, 2 A.M.

Aug. 28.—NESLE. Left bivouac at NESLE at daybreak. Retired to CRESSY. Thence to billets at MOYENCOURT. Got a mail.

Aug. 29.—Left MOYENCOURT. Took up defensive position on canal. Retired to RAGLISE thence to DIVES, arriving midnight. Met enemy's patrol. Killed 3 horses, wounded 3 men.

Aug. 30.—Left DIVES 6 A.M., marched to CLAIROIX—thence S. of COMPIEGNE 30 miles. Bivouacked there. No enemy pursued us. Got letters.

Aug. 31.—Left COMPIEGNE 5.30 A.M. and scouted to the W. 3rd Hussars being pressed, formed rearguard and covered his retreat. Bivouaced at VERBERIE, got back 8 P.M., long day. Very hot. 3rd Hussars took few prisoners.

Sept. 2.—Left VERBERIE billets 4 A.M. Big fight at NERY. Very thick fog. 1st Cavalry Brigade got caught in billets. The Bays lost very heavily, and the Royal Horse Artillery Battery nearly wiped out. HEATH (the Blues) dangerously wounded and some of C Squadron. Billeted MONTEPILLOY.

Sept. 3.—Left MONTEPILLOY billets 4 A.M. Marched South via ERMENONVILLE—LE MESNIL—AMELOT-VILLEPARISIS to LOGNES—a long hot march. Billeted in a large farm building of Menier's chocolate. CAVENDISH's Squadron returned on 4th from the reconnaissance from MONTEPILLOY. G. BUTLER dangerously wounded and 4 men; 15 men missing. They came up against enemy's Cavalry Brigade.

1st LIFE GUARDS

Sept. 4. Rest; the first since leaving London. Very hot.

Sept. 5.—Left farm at 4. Marched S.E. to BRI-COMTE—ROBERT-REAU, thence E. to Mont Farm west of MORMANT—a long tiring march. Got to farm about 9. No fighting.

Sept. 6.—Left Mont Farm 5.30. Marched N.E. to GASTINS—PECY—LE CORBIER where we billeted. Did a long day's scouting and turning enemy out of woods. The French are not up enough to push enemy back.

Sept. 7.—Left billets LE CORBIER, 5.30 A.M. Marched N.E. to DAGNY—CHEVRU—ST. REMY; our 1st, 2nd, and 3rd Infantry on our left, French Cavalry and Companies on right. First retirement of Germans. Took some prisoners. We held river line ST. SIMEON—ST. REMY. Billeted CHARTRONGES.

Sept. 8.—Left billet 5.30, took up position N.E. CHAMP LA BRIDE, covering crossing of River Petit Morin, shelling enemy, who retired N.E. to BASSEVELLE. Our 1st, 2nd, and 3rd Divisions on our left, French Companies on right; enemy retreated with loss. We crossed river and followed to BUSSIERES—BASSEVELLE under fire. Bivouacked on that line.

Sept. 9.—Left bivouac at 4, went N.E. to LA CHAPELLE, thence crossed River Marne at AZY, then N.W. to just E. of DOMPTIN. No encounter; very hot. Again bivouacked De l'Ville Farm; no transport again.

Sept. 10.—Advanced N. again. Germans still retiring. Engagement all day. Germans on line BUISSON—ST. REMY—CRAMAILLE. Our advance to BOMRES. French on our right, and 3rd Division on left. Billeted LA CROIX.

Sept. 11.—Left billets at 4, crossed River Ourcq at BRENY. Enemy retired to line SOISSONS—BRAINE. The Field Artillery in action most of day, but enemy did not stand. Poured with rain most of afternoon. Got soaked. Billeted LOUPEIGNE. Transport arrived —first now for 8 or 10 days.

Sept. 12.—Left LOUPEIGNE 5. Cold. Concentrated QUINEY then CERSEUIL. Great cannonade all along line SOISSONS—BRAINE. Evident Germans are making great stand; our 1st and 2nd Divisions are up on our right at COURCELLES and PAARS. Had a very long day, only getting into bivouac at 9 in a gale of wind and pouring rain and cold. Could get no shelter. All very miserable at VAUXTIN.

Sept. 13.—Left bivouac 3.30. Miserable, no food and all wet through. Crossed river and canal at VILLERS, all bridges blown up so had to cross by boat-bridge. Supported Royal Field Artillery at ŒUILLY. Billeted at RIVILLON very late.

Sept. 14.—Left billets 3.45, advanced to PARGNAN where all our guns and the Reserves of the 1st Division were; also Zouaves as left of French. Battle started at 5.15, and continued in intense severity till dark. Germans made two attempts to drive us out. Very wet. Billeted.

Sept. 15.—GENY. Left billets 3.40. Took up same position as yesterday. Relieved Infantry in trenching. Only shell fire before lunch. Fierce encounter along whole line. Situation much as yesterday. Billeted GENY. Again wet.

Sept. 16.—Same as yesterday. Heavy firing all along the line. Can make no impression on enemy's position. Pouring wet again. Went into GENY again.

Sept. 17.—Left billets again at 4. Position much the same. Heavy artillery fire all morning with Infantry attack in afternoon. We went into trenches all afternoon till after dark. Shelled a lot. Lost 5 men wounded; 2 horses killed, 3 wounded. Very wet.

Sept. 18.—Out as usual. Position about the same. Very heavy artillery fire all day. It turned finer in afternoon, returned to same billets. Night attack, so turned out to saddle up at 1.30 A.M. Nothing developed so turned in at 4.45.

Sept. 19.—Spent the day under the ridge at PAISSY expecting to go into trenches. Left after dark (leaving C Squadron at GENY) and marched to VAUXCERE where we arrived 11.30 P.M. 1 man and horse killed during afternoon, buried man before we left just below ridge. Wet again and our march back was not very pleasant. Roads awful and crowded. General was told of David's death.

Sept. 20.—VAUXCERE. Rest day. First since leaving MAUBEUGE a month ago. I got a bed to sleep in, so had a good sleep till 8 A.M. Wet day, spent most of my time doing orderly room, mending things and writing. F. sent 400 pipes.

Sept. 21.—Left VAUXCERE at 3, marched to our hollow at PAISSY. Dismounted for trenches in farmyard. Just got into CAVES when heavy shell fire burst all round. One in farmyard killed 8 gun horses. One of our horses killed. Got back to VAUXCERE 10 P.M.

Sept. 22.—VAUXCERE. Rest day.

Sept. 23.—Left VAUXCERE at 3 in support; did nothing. Got back at 9.30.

Sept. 24.—VAUXCERE. Rest day.

Sept. 25.—VAUXCERE. Rest day. French guns brought us stores.

Sept. 26.—The Regiment only left VAUXCERE at 3. C Squadron going to PAISSY, the others I left at the wood 1½ mile back and went on to PAISSY. Stayed there till 6.30 P.M. and returned. Hot attack all morning. Very heavy artillery fire. Got into communication with Headquarters by helio, and with Squadron. PAISSY very unpleasant in the wet. Many dead horses and some bodies about.

Sept. 27.—Rest day. Very hot. Mail.

Sept. 28.—Rest day. Dull.

Sept. 29.—Rest day. Fine.

Sept. 30.—Rest day, but as 3rd Cavalry Brigade moved billets we had to be on duty ready to saddle up. 9th Lancers got 46 casualties by big guns in LONGEPAL.

OCT. 1.—Rest day. Was President of Court of Enquiry, 1st Cavalry Brigade Headquarters. Sent in list of officers, N.C.O's I recommended to Commander-in-Chief.

Oct. 2.—Rest day, but ready to turn out at short notice. Lovely day.

Oct. 3.—Rest day, but in afternoon C Squadron and 3rd Hussars (dismounted) raided farm DE PISON and adjacent wood for supposed spies. No result. Lovely day. Went out on foot. 3rd Hussars acted as beaters and " C " Hussars mounted, piqueted wood.

Oct. 4.—Left VAUXCERE 6.30 P.M. and marched to ST. REMY, arrived there 12.30 A.M. Horses out as yards prohibited on account of glanders. Headquarters in farm house.

Oct. 5.—Left ST. REMY 6 P.M. for CREPY, 22 miles W., at 9 P.M. My Regiment ordered to return BLANZY, just north of ST. REMY to await orders. Got BLANZY 10.30 P.M. Orders midnight to go to BRAINE.

Oct. 6.—Left BLANZY 8 A.M. and BLAINE 11.30 to join 1st A.C. General DOUGLAS HAIG came and saw me and explained position. He required 1st Squadron saddled by 5.30 A.M. and to be on duty for the day.

Oct. 7.—Very quiet morning. We are in a big house (Headquarters and Blues) two in a room. Electric light. Scarcely any furniture. Horses piqueted outside under trees each side of road.

Oct. 8.—BRAINE. Rode out to CHURCH BELLEME, 1st Corps Headquarters; saw General DOUGLAS HAIG and then went out to front and had a look round. General thinks we shall be here 4 or 5 more days. Lovely day. Cold at nights.

Oct. 9.—Lovely morning; all quiet. GURNEY returned from PARIS. Situation same. Big mail.

Oct. 10.—BRAINE. A Squadron left at 9.15 A.M. for LONGUVAL to beat the surrounding woods. They returned 6 P.M. Found no enemy. At 8 P.M. B Squadron saddled up as enemy showed activity. All dined together.

Oct. 11.—Went to Headquarters. Expect to go by train to join Brigade. Sent all out for 2 hours' march. COWIE, LUXMOORE and I went long walk within 1½ miles CONDE, heard ANTWERP fell Friday.

Oct. 12.—BRAINE. French 1st Corps on our right. Lost 600 men in ten minutes in an attack early this morning. Run up against a wall of machine guns. Lovely day.

Oct. 13.—BRAINE. Heavy gunning about 7 P.M., so saddled up 1st Squadron. Quiet again, 9 P.M.

Oct. 14.—BRAINE. Went up to Headquarters. Likely to move to-morrow. Orders to move came, 6 P.M.

Oct. 15.—Left BRAINE. Marched A Squadron, Headquarters and C Squadron by two trains from NEUILLY ST. FRONT 9.50 P.M., and 11.50 A.M.; B Squadron from FERE-EN-TARDENOIS 8.50 P.M. Arrived ST. DENIS 7 A.M. There watered and had breakfast in train.

Oct. 16.—Arrived AMIENS 4 P.M. Watered and fed in train. BOULOGNE 7.30 P.M., CALAIS 9.30 P.M., HAZEBROUCK our destination, where we expect to arrive in morning.

Oct. 17.—Train arrived HAZEBROUCK 8 A.M. Detrained. Went into town and field. Orders to proceed KEMMEL at 2.30 P.M.; arrived KEMMEL 6 P.M. 2nd Cavalry Division there. Saw General VAUGHAN who advised me to go on to farm Cross roads 1 mile W.N.W. of MESSINES as our Brigade was there. Arrived 8 P.M. Transport 11 P.M.

Oct. 18.—Marched into MESSINES 10 A.M. Squadrons billeted farms. I in town. Saw Brigade fighting about WARNETON. We are in 2nd Cavalry Division. GOUGH saw Brigade after dinner about position to take up in morning.

Oct. 19.—Left MESSINES for position about HALTE. Relieved 5th and in trenches 5.30 A.M. Dug ourselves in as best we could. 3rd Hussars on our left and 5th Dragoon Guards on right. Good deal of shelling. Stayed in trenches all night.

Oct. 21.—In trenches. Attack expected by enemy from WARNETON. Developed rapidly, heavy shelling and enfilade fire. 3rd Hussars had to fall back. Enemy enfiladed our left flank. CAVENDISH killed. TROTTER, MURRAY, SMITH, WALLACE, COMBE, 45 N.C.O.'s and men wounded.

Oct. 22.—Dug ourselves in all morning. ASTOR and I got hit by shell at 2. Got moved at 7. Motor Ambulance to BAILLEUL. Stayed in BAILLEUL hospital. F. GUEST, B. LAMBTON, and SIR JOHN FRENCH came in afternoon. F. G. motored me to BOULOGNE. Arrived on board hospital ship "Carisbrooke Castle" 8 P.M. Boat left at 10 P.M.

1st LIFE GUARDS

Extract from Private Diary of
Surgeon-Major COWIE, 1st Life Guards.

Oct. 21.—Regiment holding trenches on high ground 1 mile E. by N. of MESSINES on the Messines road, by a windmill. The right of the Regiment lay close to windmill which stood on a round grassed mound; the mill itself was entirely of wood resting on a single pedestal also of wood. The Germans occasionally shelled this mill. One of the shells (shrapnel) wounded the C.O. on the leg, Captain ASTOR elbow, Corporal MOORE stomach, Trooper TOBIN back, and another. Otherwise a quiet day. A light ambulance wagon was brought up past the farm at the rear of the position and the wounded were removed to WYTSCHAETE where they were transferred to a motor ambulance.

Oct. 22.—Regiment in same position, Major LORD CRICHTON commanding. Heavy firing all the early morning before daylight on left of our position. The Germans could be seen digging on the low ground on the left front. J Battery shelled them to some effect from S. of WYTSCHAETE. Murray SMITH, who was left in a trench near WARNETON on 20th, is in the hands of the Saxons who are known to be gentlemen (he was taken to hospital at LILLE the same day, and after doing very well for some days, died just when he was going to be moved to a private house).

Oct. 23.—The wooden windmill has disappeared from the landscape, being knocked to bits by high explosive. J Battery again shelled trenches on our left front where the Germans were apparently mounting 2 machine guns. This evening the Regiment was relieved by the "Wild's Rifles" of the LAHORE Division, and went into billets at a farm three-quarters mile N. of WYTSCHAETE on the W. and GROSSE VIERSTRAAT road.

Oct. 24.—Regiment resting at the farm. An officer rode over to see the Headquarter Cavalry Brigade at ZANDVOORDE and brought back news of the Regiment there. BRASSEY was in command as C.O. had gone sick. There was constant sniping at the Headquarters of the Blues and 2nd Life Guards behind the trenches at ZANDVOORDE.

Oct. 25.—A real fine morning—everyone enjoying a spell off. Some officers rode over to ZANDVOORDE to see the Regiment.

Oct. 26.—Regiment moved out into trenches E. of MESSINES again. The horses were taken up to a farm half mile behind the trenches, with the result that they came under an accurate shrapnel fire which killed one horse and wounded nearly a score in as many seconds. By lucky chance not a man was hurt. This night our new machine-gun officer, CALEDON, went sick with fever.

Oct. 27.—Messines Church burnt to the ground and many farms, too, were alight this evening. Regiment relieved from the trenches and went back to billets at the farm, N. of WYTSCHAETE.

Oct. 28.—Rumours this morning of the Regiment being broken up. Everyone very sad about it as we are most uncommonly happy. Some of us rode to YPRES and explored the Cathedral, and saw some fine French Infantry marching through to the North.

Oct. 29.—Regiment "standing by" at the farm were called out in support to the N.E. of VYTOCHAETE near the CHATEAU HOLLELIKE. We waited with the Greys on the WYTSCHAETE—ST. ELOI road by the lodge of the Chateau—back to the farm at nightfall. To-night rumour says the Regiment is to be broken up when opportunity occurs.

Oct. 30.—This morning the Regiment was called out in support of the 3rd Brigade, and on this evening went into trenches at WYTSCHAETE on the E. of the town.

Oct. 31.—Regiment in the trenches E. of WYTSCHAETE, 1st Life Guards Squadron on the right of the line, the machine gun holding the extreme of their flank at the Cross roads to MESSINES (S.) and OOSTAVERNE (E.), the trenches running along the Eastern or farther side of the ST. ELOI road. There were a few casualties in the evening—Trooper LEWRY being killed, IMPLETON and two others wounded. All day the high explosive shells were bursting over WYTSCHAETE, especially directed at the wood N.W. and the KEMMEL road. At nightfall incendiary shells came whizzbanging into the village.

Before midnight the enemy could be heard making a great noise on our left front, blowing horns, playing bands and shouting, they could be seen later passing across our front from N.E., and they fell upon our right-hand trenches held by the 1st Life Guards' Squadron.

The enemy gained a footing here, but a counter attack was ordered and our men, who got into the trenches again, led by Lieutenant LEIGH and Lieutenant SMITH (Captain WYNDHAM being wounded), did some execution among the Germans, many of whom appeared very young.

Nov. 1.—The enemy, however, were in too great strength, and we fell back through WYTSCHAETE in the direction of KEMMEL. During this retirement, before we had got clear of WYTSCHAETE,

Major Lord Crichton and Lieutenant Smith were lost, and Lieutenant Leigh was wounded. Some of the Lincolns had come up in support in the early morning and helped to check the enemy's advance, which, however, was never pressed beyond the outskirts of W. in the Kemmel direction.

The 5th N. Fusiliers came up and dug themselves in on the Eastern slope of a ridge 1½ miles W. of Wytschaete where the English trenches have remained ever since.

This evening the Regiment went into billets near La Clyte, a draft having joined with Captain Stubber and other officers.

Nov. 2.—Regiment in support all day—many shells falling on Mt. Kemmel—went into billets at Cross roads, 1 mile S. of Bailleul.

Nov. 3.—Regiment moved to Fontaine Hoek, 1 mile W. of the Metiren—Bailleul road and rested there until

Nov. 7, when they marched out to take over the trenches at Walverghem, leaving the horses in a field 1 mile on the Bailleul side of Neuve Eglise. As the Brigade (dismounted) passed through Neuve Eglise at dusk some well aimed shells caused a few casualties, a Carbineer being killed and Corporal Coxhead (since dead) 2nd Life Guards' Squadron being among the wounded.

Nov. 8.—Regiment holding trenches at Walverghem. There was a good deal of shelling of the country behind the trenches where two French batteries were in action. The small cottage chosen for a dressing station fared badly, and four of the horses of the Medical Staff were wounded (two having to be shot).

Nov. 9.—There was heavy shelling at times, and the farm used by Headquarters at night was set alight and burned furiously. We had two or three casualties. In the evening went into billets near Sveinwerke.

Nov. 10th.—Our Commanding Officer, Captain Gurney, went sick, leaving us in command of Captain Bowlby (since killed).

Nov. 11. Regiment marched to Ypres under command of Captain Bowlby, Royal Horse Guards, and joined the Headquarters' Cavalry Brigade at dusk near Veloren Hoek—" the muddy farm." The Headquarters' Cavalry Brigade were then doing "Fire Brigade." No sooner had we reached the muddy farm and night fallen than a sudden order came for the Brigade to turn out: Composite Regiment, "Every man to his own Regiment"; and struggling over the broken country in pitchy darkness, a cataract of rain, heavy squalls of wind and oceans of mud the Composite Regiment disappeared and was absorbed into the 7th Cavalry Brigade.

WAR DIARY OF

WAR DIARY of 1st LIFE GUARDS.
FIRST YEAR, 1914—1915.

Kept by Captain the Hon. E. H. WYNDHAM.

Zeebrugge—Oct. 8, 1914, 6 A.M.—Headquarters and 1 Squadron (D) disembarked, and remained awaiting orders on the quay till 3.30 p.m. Then marched slowly through BLANKENBERGHE. The column was considerably delayed in the streets of the town owing to non-receipt of orders. This was unfortunate as it led to the ranks being considerably broken by inhabitants offering hospitality. It seems undesirable for troops to remain halted in friendly towns.

Blankenberghe—Oct. 8, 6 P.M.—Orders received through Officer Commanding 2nd Life Guards to bivouac for the night. This was carried out on the shore half-a-mile West of the town.

Blankenberghe—Oct. 9, 5 A.M.—Stood to arms at dawn.

Blankenberghe—Oct. 9, 8 A.M.—Received orders to be at JABBEKE at 10.30, in accordance with Brigade Orders.

OPERATION ORDERS NO. 1.

By Brigadier-General C. M. KAVANAGH, C.V.O., C.B., D.S.O.,
Commanding 7th Cavalry Brigade.

(*Reference Map. Scale 1" to 3.95 miles.*)

S.S. "SEPTAH," OSTEND,
October 8th, 1914.

ORDER NO. 1.—German Cavalry is reported south of line OOSTVLETEREN—MERCKEM—ROULERS. Belgian troops on the line DIXMUDE—ROULERS—THIELT, with detachments at THOUROUT and COOLSCAMP. Belgian and French troops are at GHENT and BRUGES.

2.—The 3rd Cavalry Division will take up a line of protection from GHENT exclusive to OSTEND inclusive, facing South. The 6th Cavalry Brigade will occupy the general line of the railway from GHENT exclusive to ST. GEORGES inclusive. Brigade Headquarters at RONSELE.

3.—The 7th Cavalry Brigade will hold the line from ST. GEORGES exclusive to OUDENBURG, with Brigade Headquarters at BRUGES.

4.—The 1st Life Guards will concentrate by 10.30 a.m. at JABBEKE, and will hold the line from OUDENBURG to the BRUGES—THOUROUT Railway about LOPHEM exclusive.

The Royal Horse Guards will concentrate at BRUGES at 10.30 a.m., and will hold the line from the BRUGES—THOUROUT Railway about LOPHEM inclusive to ST. GEORGES exclusive. Protective patrols, strength half a troop, will be sent to the line ST. PIERRE CAPELLE—THOUROUT—WYNGHENE, the BRUGES—THOUROUT Railway being the dividing line between regiments.

Regiments will report position of their Headquarters to Brigade Headquarters.

1st LIFE GUARDS

The 2nd Life Guards will be at BRUGES in reserve at 10.30 a.m.

Divisional Headquarters will be at BRUGES.

5.—Dressing Stations will be open at RONSELE and the Railway Station at BRUGES.

6.—The 3rd Signal Squadron will establish a post of 3 motor-cyclists at KNESSELACRE Road Junction by 3 p.m. to-morrow.

7.—Mobile Stations will be open at RONSELE and the Railway Station at BRUGES by the A.V.C.

8.—Two days' supplies will be delivered by motor at Regimental Headquarters to-morrow afternoon.

9.—Reports to the Southern Lock Bridge at Ostend until 10.30 a.m., afterwards to BRUGES Post Office.

N. NEILL, Captain,
Brigade-Major, 7th Cavalry Brigade.

Issued at 12.30 a.m., 9th October, 1914.

Copies to :—
Officer Commanding 1st Life Guards.
    ,,   ,,   C Squadron 1st Life Guards.
    ,,   ,,   Royal Horse Guards.
    ,,   ,,   2nd Life Guards.
    ,,   ,,   Signal Troop.
Supply Officer.

Owing to cobbled roads rate of progress was slow. Destination not reached till 11.30. Two Squadrons (A and C) who had disembarked at OSTEND the previous day rejoined Headquarters.

Jabbeke—Oct. 9, 12.35 P.M.—Message received :—

B.M.I.
To 1st Life Guards, Jabbeke.

"The rôle of protecting the Railway has ceased. The Brigade will go into billets in area LOPHEM, OOSTCAMP, OEDELEM, SYSSEELE. Your regiment probably in two first-named villages. Billeting parties should meet Staff-Captain at bridge over Canal in BRUGES on BRUGES-OOSTCAMP road at 1 p.m."

From 7th Cavalry Brigade, Bruges, 11.40 a.m.   N. NEILL, Captain Brigade Major.

Lophem—Oct. 9, 5.30 P.M.—Squadrons reached their billeting places.

Lophem—Oct. 10, 5 A.M.—Stood to arms. At 7 a.m., Operation Order No. 2 received :—

OPERATION ORDERS NO. 2.

By Brigadier-General C. M. KAVANAGH, C.V.O., C.B., D.S.O.

BRUGES,
October 9th, 1914.

1.—It is understood that there are considerable forces of the enemy in the neighbourhood of YPRES. Fighting has taken place to-day East of GHENT in which it is believed that the Allies have been successful. The 3rd Cavalry Division will remain in its present billets to-morrow.

2.—The Officer Commanding 2nd Life Guards will detail an officer's patrol in accordance with instructions issued.

3.—Regiments will send empty wagons to the Goods' Station at BRUGES to draw two days' rations.

Royal Horse Guards .. .. 10 a.m.
2nd Life Guards .. .. 11 a.m.
1st Life Guards .. .. 12 noon.

Sufficient fatigue parties for loading and drawing will accompany wagons.

4.—Reports to the Bridge at the southern border of BRUGES on the OOSTCAMP road.

N. NEILL, Captain,
Brigade-Major, 7th Cavalry Brigade.

Issued 10 p.m.

Copies to :—

1st Life Guards.	Supply Officer.
2nd Life Guards.	A.D.C.
Royal Horse Guards.	B.M.
Signal Troop.	War Diary.

WAR DIARY OF

Lophem—Oct. 10, 5 A.M.—Lieutenant C. D. Leyland took a patrol to THOUROUT. Report:—

To 7th Cavalry Brigade.

"Patrol from THOUROUT reports place clear of enemy and occupied by BELGIANS. BELGIAN Officer reports following at YPRES—25 GERMAN cyclists and cavalry. At DICKEBUSCH few GERMANS on road bridge. At KEMMELL and NEUVE EGLISE large force of GERMANS. LILLE is reported to be barricaded by the enemy."

From 1st Life Guards, Lophem Castle, 9.15 a.m.   E. H. WYNDHAM, Captain and Adjutant.

This report was the first news received of the enemy.

Lophem—Oct. 10, 12 NOON.—Orders received for Brigade to assemble at BEERNEM. March there considerably delayed at OOSTCAMP by large bodies of BELGIAN artillery retiring from GHENT and ANTWERP on the same road.

Beernem—Oct. 10, 2.30 P.M.—Reached destination. Orders then received to go into billets at RUDDERVOORDE. On reaching this place it was found to be crowded with BELGIAN troops, so regiment bivouacked 1½ miles S. of village at the CHATEAU at 6 p.m.

Ruddervoorde—Oct. 11, 5 A.M.—Brigade Orders:—

OPERATION ORDERS NO. 3.
By Brigadier-General C. M. KAVANAGH, C.V.O., C.B., D.S.O.,
Commanding 7th Cavalry Brigade.

RUDDERVOORDE,
October 10th, 1914.

1.—Fighting has taken place to-day round GHENT. Enemy retired in S.W. direction. A mixed force of cavalry reported at LOKEREN. GERMAN Cavalry Division reported to-day at WARNETON (D.G.).

2.—The Brigade will remain in present billets.

3.—The Officer Commanding 2nd Life Guards will detail one Squadron to take up a line of observation by 7 a.m. from railway due West of LICHTERVEDE (inclusive), through SWEYESEELE to WYNGHENE. Squadron Leader to report to Brigade Headquarters at 6.15 a.m. for further instructions.

4.—The Officer Commanding Royal Horse Guards will detail one Squadron for reconnaissance. The Squadron Leader to report at Brigade Headquarters at 7 a.m.

N. NEILL, Captain,
Brigade-Major.

Issued 11.15 p.m.
Copies to:—
    1st Life Guards.   A.D.C.
    2nd Life Guards.   B.M.
    Blues.   Diary.
    Signal Troop.

Saddled up 5 a.m. and stood to arms till 7 a.m. 5.15 a.m. 2 officers' patrols were sent out in accordance with orders received from Brigade Headquarters. One under Lt. Hon. W. R. Wyndham to THIELT via EEGHEM. One under Lt. Lord Somers to cross-roads 1 mile west of railway at RITTHEM. They reported all clear.

To General Officer Commanding 7th Cavalry Brigade, Chateau 2 miles S. of Ruddevoorde (Sunday):—

"BELGIAN officer reports on the 9th inst. a regiment of BAVARIAN Cavalry N. of MENIN line DADISEELE—LEDEGHEM with patrols between COMINES and MENIN. An engagement took place between FRENCH all arms and GERMAN force, strength 15,000, 100 canons, 50 mitrailleuses at BAILLEUL; the GERMANS retired direction of LILLE. Telephone communication now restored to YPRES and COURTRAI. The bridges over River LYS at MENIN and COURTRAI, partially destroyed by GERMANS, are still passable for cavalry and transport. Country S.E. of line COURTRAI—PETEGEM is clear of enemy."

From O.C. No. 1 patrol, A Squad. 1st Life Guards, Ritthem, 7.45 a.m.   SOMERS, Lieut.

1st LIFE GUARDS

To 7th Cavalry Brigade.

"I communicated with General in command at THIELT and he told me there were no GERMANS on line ROULERS, INGELMUNSTER to DEYNZE."

THIELT.

W. R. WYNDHAM, Lieut.

Ruddervoorde—Oct. 12, 8 A.M.—At 8 a.m. regiment left as A.G. to Brigade. Marched through COOLSCAMP to ISEGHEM. At ISEGHEM received orders to march to DE GOD via BOSCHMOLLEN to take up protective line MOORSLEDE—LENDELEDE, with patrols to line 5 miles S. of these places.

OPERATION ORDERS NO. 4.

By Brigadier-General C. M. KAVANAGH, C.V.O., C.B., D.S.O.,
Commanding 7th Cavalry Brigade.

CHATEAU DE RUDDERVOORDE,
October 12th, 1914.

1.—The 7th Division fought a successful action in the neighbourhood of GHENT yesterday and captured many prisoners. The armed Motor-cars attached to 3rd Cavalry Division made a successful reconnaissance.

2.—The 3rd Cavalry Division will take up a line of protection to-day. 6th Cavalry Brigade ZONNEBEKE—MOORSLEDE (both inclusive). 7th Cavalry Brigade MOORSLEDE (exclusive)—LENDELEDE (F. 8) inclusive. Our 7th Division will be at THIELT with a detachment at COOLSCAMP.

3.—The Brigade will march *via* SWEVEZEELE—COOLSCAMP—ARDOYE—ISEGHEM to RUMBEKE. Advanced guard, 1st Life Guards. Main body will pass the gate of the Chateau de RUDDERVOORDE (billet of Brigade Headquarters) as follows:—

    Brigade Headquarters and Signal Troop 8.15 a.m.
    Royal Horse Guards   8.15 a.m.
    Second Life Guards   8.20 a.m.
    2nd Echelon Transport in order of march
      of Regiments   8.30 a.m.

4.—Billeting Parties will meet the Staff Captain at ISEGHEM at 12 noon.

5.—Empty wagons will be sent to RUMBEKE to draw supplies when notified.

6.—Reports during march to head of main body. Afterwards to RUMBEKE.

N. NEILL, Captain,
Brigade-Major, 7th Cavalry Brigade.

Issued 6 a.m.
Copies to:—
    1st Life Guards.   Transport Officer.
    Blues.   Staff Captain.
    2nd Life Guards.   Brigade-Major.
    Signal Troop.   A.D.C.
    Supply Officer.

SPECIAL INSTRUCTIONS TO OFFICER COMMANDING ADVANCED GUARD.

1.—After arrival at RUMBEKE you will occupy to line of protection referred to in Operation Orders, paragraph 2, pushing patrols to the line DADIZEELE—HEULE.

2.—A GERMAN Cavalry Regiment was reported in DADIZEELE yesterday and an Infantry Division S. of GHELUWE.

N. NEILL, Captain, Brigade-Major.

October 12th, 1914.

Reports received:—

To 1st Life Guards, Cross Roads, ¼ mile North of DE GOD.

"Have occupied LENDELEDE and sent patrols down all roads running SOUTH in my Section—my advanced guard was fired at by a BELGIAN Cyclist patrol from Southern side of LENDELEDE, one horse hit in quarter. BELGIAN Officer in charge of patrol reports all clear round COURTRAI in the immediate vicinity. SWEVEGHEM S.E. of COURTRAI and HEULE still in telephonic communication with COURTRAI. BELGIAN Officer also reports six armoured motors at GHELUWE."

From C. Squad., 1st Life Guards, Lendelede, 3.5 p.m.

H. GROSVENOR, Capt.

To O.C. 1st Life Guards, Cross Roads, North of DE GOD (Ref. Sheet 5).

"Have occupied line as ordered. BELGIAN Officer reports he has platoons Cyclists at PASSCHENDAELE D. 8—DADIZEELE and WINKEL ST. ELOI, both E. 8 Sheet I. These appear to be withdrawing. Accommodation for 60 horses on farm ¼ mile from here in VELDMOLEN, and room for others scattered about. Can billet here comfortably."

From A. Squadron, Veldmolen Cross Roads, 4.50.

L. H. HARDY, Capt.

WAR DIARY OF

De God—Oct. 12, 6 p.m.—At 6 p.m. retired into bivouac at RUMBEKE. A squadron on outpost from ROULERS—MENIN road to cross-roads ½ mile S.E. of bivouac.

Rumbeke—Oct. 13, 7 a.m.—At 7 a.m. in accordance with Operation Order No. 6, Regiment marched to YPRES, thence on MENIN via GHELUWE.

OPERATION ORDERS NO. 5.*
By Brigadier-General C. M. KAVANAGH, C.V.O., C.B., D.S.O.,
Commanding 7th Household Cavalry Brigade.

RUMBEKE,
October 12th, 1914.

1.—GERMAN Forces are reported as under :—
    2,000 at SOTTEGEM (1. 8).
    1 BAVARIAN Cavalry Division at WARNETON (D. 9).
    20,000 at TOURNAI.
    20,000 at HAZEBROUCK (B. 9).
    A heavy battle was proceeding this morning between ARMENTIERES and LILLE.

2.—The 3rd Cavalry Division will occupy the protective line detailed in Brigade Order No. 2 of Operation Orders No. 4 of October 12, 1914, by 6 a.m. to-morrow and will push forward patrols to the line on the River Lys. The 7th Cavalry Brigade will be responsible for the reconnaissance area east of and including the ROULERS—MENIN road.

3.—Regiments will be responsible for the line as follows :—
    2nd Life Guards from MOORSLEDE (exclusive) to the ISEGHAM—WINKEL ST. ELOI road exclusive.
    Royal Horse Guards with 1 Squadron from the ISEGHEM—WINKEL ST. ELOI road to LENDELEDE both inclusive, with a detachment of 1 Troop at INGELMUNSTER. Remainder of the Regiment in support at BOSCHMOLENS.
    1st Life Guards having recalled their posts now out at 6 a.m. will remain at RUMBEKE in reserve.

4.—Reports to RUMBEKE.

N. NEILL, Captain,
Brigade-Major, 7th Household Cavalry Brigade.

Issued at 9.30 p.m.
    Copies to :—
        1st Life Guards.   7th Signal Troop.
        2nd Life Guards.   Brigade Major.
        Royal Horse Guards.   A.D.C.

OPERATION ORDERS NO. 6.
By Brigadier-General C. M. KAVANAGH, C.V.O., C.B., D.S.O.,
Commanding 7th Cavalry Brigade.

RUMBEKE,
October 13th, 1914.

1.—GOUGH's Cavalry Division captured MONTS DES CATS last evening, 10 miles South-West of YPRES.

2.—The 3rd Cavalry Division will march to-day to join up with the 2nd Cavalry Division. The 6th Brigade will march *via* OOSTNIEUWKERKE and the second A in PASSCHENDAELE to YPRES. The 7th Cavalry Brigade will march *via* MOORSLEDE and ZONNEBEKE to YPRES.

3.—Units will be ready to march at 7 a.m. 2nd Life Guards will find an advance guard of 2 squadrons and left flank guard of 1 squadron. Order of march of main body : Royal Horse Guards, 1st Life Guards. 1st Life Guards will fall in behind the Royal Horse Guards at the Cross Roads Pt. 11, 3 miles South of ROULERS.

4.—The 2nd Echelon Transport will follow the column in order of march of Regiments, that of the Royal Horse Guards will halt at the Cross Roads immediately North of DE GOD to allow that of the 2nd Life Guards to go in front. Transport of Brigade Headquarters and 1st Life Guards will join the rear at the Cross Roads Pt. 11.

5.—Reports to head of main body.

N. NEILL, Captain,
Brigade-Major, 7th Cavalry Brigade.

Issued at 5.45 a.m.
    Copies to :—
        1st Life Guards.
        2nd Life Guards.   Transport Officer.
        Royal Horse Guards   Brigade Major.
        7th Signal Troop.   Staff Captain.
            Supply Officer.   A.D.C.

* Operation Orders No. 5 cancelled by No. 6.

1st LIFE GUARDS

MENIN was reported held by the enemy, and Brigade prepared to drive them out, when Divisional Order was received for an immediate retirement to billets. Regiment was ordered to march to WINKEL ST. ELOI, via DADIZEELE. Small hostile patrol encountered on the way.

Winkel St. Eloi—Oct. 13, 8 P.M.—On arrival at WINKEL ST. ELOI, an urgent order was received from the Division to escort K Battery R.H.A. to ISEGHEM. Arrived there 9 p.m. Headquarters A and D Squadrons settled into billets by midnight. C Squadron were detached all day to protect Divisional Headquarters first at ROULERS and subsequently East of ISEGHEM. Wagons arrived at 2 a.m. Were ordered to fill up here, but missed supply column.

Iseghem—Oct. 13-14, MIDNIGHT.—Operation Order No. 7 received:—

OPERATION ORDERS NO. 7.
By Brigadier-General C. M. KAVANAGH, C.V.O., C.B., D.S.O.,
Commanding 7th Cavalry Brigade.
WINKEL ST. ELOI,
October 13th, 1914.

1.—It is reported that a hostile force is S. of YPRES. The 4th Corps will advance to YPRES in order to attack enemy's right flank in co-operation with our 2nd and 3rd Corps. The 3rd Cavalry Division will march on DADIZEELE, 6th Cavalry Brigade leading.

2.—7th Cavalry Brigade will pass starting point in WINKEL ST. ELOI village at 5 a.m. Order of march:—
    2nd Life Guards.
    Blues.
    1st Life Guards.

3.—1st Echelon G.S. wagons will follow the Brigade under command of Captain NAPER, Royal Horse Guards. 2nd Echelon in order of march will follow 1st Echelon.

4.—The 2nd Life Guards will furnish an A.G. of 1 Squadron.

5.—Reports to head of main body.

Issued 12 midnight.

12.35 A.M.—Order received from Divisional Headquarters. C Squadron was told off for this duty.

To Officer Commanding 1st Life Guards,
    ISEGHEM.

"The 7th Division leaves ROULERS at 6 a.m. to-day. You will please detail one Squadron as a left flank guard to the 7th Division, during its march. On completion of its mission, this Squadron will report to Officer Commanding 7th Cavalry Brigade at YPRES.
"The remainder of your Regiment will march as per instructions already issued by 7th Cavalry Brigade."
M. F. GAGE, Lieut.-Colonel.

ISEGHEM,
12.35 a.m. *October 14th*, 1914.

3.30 a.m. Headquarters and A and D Squadrons marched to join Brigade at WINKEL ST. ELOI.

Ypres—Oct. 14, 10 A.M.—Arrived at YPRES and halted till midday. During halt GERMAN Taube Monoplane flew over the town, was fired at by Maxims from armoured motors and brought down. At noon moved in accordance with Order:—

WAR DIARY OF

To ALL UNITS,
   B.M.1.

1.—The enemy's cavalry is reported on all roads S.W., S. and S.E. of YPRES.

2.—The 6th Cavalry Brigade will advance at 10.30 a.m. towards the line LA CLYTE—KEMMEL—WYTSCHAETE.

3.—The 7th Cavalry Brigade and Royal Horse Artillery will advance at 12 noon towards GROOTE VIERSTRAAT.

4.—The Officer Commanding Royal Horse Guards will detail one Squadron as advanced Guard.

Order of march of main body :—

    Signal Squadron.
    Royal Horse Guards.
    Royal Horse Artillery.
    1st Life Guards.
    2nd Life Guards.

5.—The Officer Commanding 2nd Life Guards will leave one Squadron at YPRES.

6.—2nd Echelon Transport will remain at YPRES. G.S. Wagons 1st Echelon will follow the Brigade.

7.—Reports to head of main body.
                    N. NEILL, Captain,
                    Brigade-Major, 7th Cavalry Brigade.
        YPRES, 11.15 a.m.

During the advance a battle could be heard raging on our front beyond KEMMEL. This was believed to be Generals GOUGH and ALLENBY endeavouring to effect a junction with the Division, in which they were successful, General CHETWODE's Brigade billeting in KEMMEL. Regiment billeted in farms round GROOT VIERSTRAAT at 6 p.m. Wagons arrived 9 p.m. They had been unable to fill up during the day, but supply column arrived shortly after.

Groote Vierstraat—Oct. 14, 11 P.M.—C Squadron arrived in billets on completion of their rôle of left flank guard to 7th Division. In addition they reported verbally having inflicted loss on the enemy.

    To 1st Life Guards.
    C Squad. 1.
    " What are orders regarding protection to-night ? We had some small engagements with Uhlans to-day. Found GHELUWE occupied by about 30 GERMANS, attacked dismounted with two troops and ousted them, regret to say Corporal of H. LEGGETT killed. Pte. EDWARDS sent to ROULERS to hospital early this morning with bad rheumatism."
    10.25 p.m.   H. GROSVENOR, Capt.

Groote Vierstraat—Oct. 15.—Remained in billets. Brigadier-General BINGHAM visited Regiment. Lieutenant R. C. BINGHAM left to join Headquarters 4th Cavalry Brigade.

Groote Vierstraat—Oct. 16.—Marched at 7.40 a.m. (A Squadron A.G. to Brigade via YPRES to POELCAPPELLE Station. Patrols under Lieutenant Hon. G. WARD and Lieutenant Sir P. BROCKLEHURST sent out from POELCAPPELLE to STADEN, one by East and one by West. One by East under Sir P. BROCKLEHURST met the enemy on outskirts of STADEN, came under close fire of M.G. and lost one man killed (Tr. HENLEY).

1st LIFE GUARDS

OPERATION ORDERS NO. 8.

By Brigadier-General C. M. KAVANAGH, C.V.O., C.B., D.S.O.,
Commanding 7th Cavalry Brigade.

GROOT VIERSTRAAT,
October 16th, 1914.

Reference Map 1:100,000. *Ostend.*

1.—The Cavalry Corps is roughly on the line NEUVE EGLISE—WYTSCHAETE. The 7th Division is about YPRES.

The GERMANS are reported to be entrenching both sides of the LYS Canal.

2.—The 3rd Cavalry Division will occupy the general line POELCAPPELLE Station—ST. JULIAN (2 miles N.W. of ZONNEBEKE).

3.—The Brigade will march *via* PLAS and YPRES to POELCAPPELLE. Advanced Guard 1 Squadron, 1st Life Guards.

Units in order of march will pass the Cross Roads ¾ mile N.N.E. of GROOTE VIERSTRAAT as follows :—

Brigade Headquarters and Signal Troop	7.40 a.m.
1st Life Guards (less 1 Squadron)	7.40 a.m.
2nd Life Guards	7.45 a.m.
Royal Horse Guards	7.55 a.m.
Field Ambulance	8.0 a.m.
G.S. wagons, 1st Echelon	8.0 a.m.
2nd Echelon	8.5 a.m.

4.—The head will halt at WIELTJE on the YPRES—POELCAPPELLE Road, where instructions for the further advance will be given.

5.—Reports to the head of main body.

N. NEILL, Captain,
Brigade-Major, 7th Cavalry Brigade.

Issued at 5.15 a.m.

Copies to :—
1st Life Guards.
2nd Life Guards.
Royal Horse Guards.
Field Ambulance.
Signal Troop.

Supply Officer.
Transport Officer.
Brigade Major.
A.D.C.
Staff Captain.

Poelcappelle Station—Oct. 16, 3 P.M.—With reference to B.M.3 16th, messages received from A. G.

B.M.3.

To 1st Life Guards, POELCAPPELLE Station.

"Brigade advancing to OOSTNIEUWKERKE to confirm report as to presence of enemy. You remain where you are and patrol well to your right flank and watch for opportunity to attack enemy retiring on DIXMUDE road."

From 7th Cavalry Brigade, POELCAPPELLE, 1 P.M.

No. 1.

"Centre section on main road reports 150 of enemy advancing down main road through the OU in FORET DE HOUTHULST. Two Troops (A Squadron) and BELGIAN Cyclists are at 3 on map. Two Troops of Captain STANLEY's Squadron are in support. Enemy estimated three kilos distant."

From 1st Life Guards, Cross Roads on Main Road, ½ mile N. of POELCAPPELLE Station.

2.50 P.M.
L. H. HARDY, Captain.

No. 2.

To O.C. 1st Life Guards, POELCAPPELLE Station.

"Think enemy's patrols have turned W. on HOUTHULST—MERREM road. BELGIAN Cavalry patrol reports 80 of enemy's Cavalry feeding at CLERCKEN. Am pushing out patrols to N. and N.W. again to try and get into touch and more definite information. In excellent concealed position if they do come on, but fear they won't."

3.30.
L. H. HARDY, Captain.

No engagement with enemy ensued. Brigade billeted at PASSCHENDEALE at 9.30 p.m.

Passchendeale—Oct. 17th.—Two squadrons made reconnaissances and remained on outpost in farms 1 mile E. of village.

WAR DIARY OF

OPERATION ORDERS NO. 9.

By Brigadier-General C. M. KAVANAGH, C.V.O., C.B., D.S.O.,
Commanding 7th Cavalry Brigade.

PASSCHENDEALE,
October 17th, 1914.

1.—The troops will remain in present billets.

2.—The 6th Cavalry Brigade will observe the MENIN—ROULERS road.

3.—The Officer Commanding 1st Life Guards will detail 1 Squadron to march at 6 a.m. to the Cross Roads on the STADEN—ROULERS and WESTROOSEBEKE—HOOGLEDE road. The Squadron Leader to report to Brigade Headquarters at 5.45 a.m. for instructions. The Officer Commanding 2nd Life Guards will detail an Officer to accompany this Squadron.

4.—The 2nd Life Guards will maintain touch with the BELGIAN Cavalry Division about STADENBURG.

5.—Remainder of troops to be saddled up at 6 a.m. Protective Patrols will be despatched at 5.30 a.m. as follows :—

    1st Life Guards to MAGERMERIE.

    2nd Life Guards to OOSTNIEUWKERKE.

    Royal Horse Guards to MOORSLEDE.

N. NEILL, Captain,
Brigade-Major, 7th Cavalry Brigade.

Issued at 8.30 p.m.
Copies to :—
1st Life Guards.
2nd Life Guards.
Royal Horse Guards.
Signal Troop.
Field Ambulance.

A.D.C.
Brigade-Major.
Transport Officer.
Supply Officer.

At midnight patrol went out of which report is :—

To O.C. 1st Life Guards.

"The evening of the 17th, Trs. HIBBERD and HAYDEN and myself were sent on a night patrol to verify a report that some of the enemy were in a chateau 1 mile East of PASSCHENDEALE. A telephone message was sent to the Station to warn the Blues that the patrol was going through there. On the way we noticed a man standing in the road who looked suspicious, and noticed his dress and appearance. On reaching the Blues' post I learnt that Station was in GERMAN hands. We therefore had to go across country towards Chateau. After creeping about 300 yards, saw sentry on Cross Roads 500 yards S. of Chateau, also lamp-signalling at corner of wood S.W. of Chateau. On moving forward heard someone running up over plough behind. He would have fallen over me had he come on. He was making for signalling lamp at corner of wood. I caught him and prevented him calling out, and left him bound and gagged, apparently dead. We then crossed road as sentry walked away, and advanced on Chateau. Noticed lights in wood and heard horses also mounted man moving along road E. from wood, could go no further as pickets in front and both sides were alert, returned different way and reported to Brigadier."

From Officer Commanding reconnoitring Patrol A Squadron, Passchendeale, October 18th,

12.50 a.m.

SOMERS, Lieut.

In accordance with this report A Squadron went out at 5.30 a.m. and found report was correct, but bulk of enemy left just before they arrived, and they were only able to fire on a belated patrol at 700 yards range. They captured one horse and wounded 3.

Passchendeale—Oct. 18, 6 A.M.—Brigade marched at 6 a.m. to Pt. 29, 1 mile S. of OOSTNIEUWKERKE, C Squadron was detailed as right flank guard to Brigade, and D Squadron were sent on a reconnaissance to cross-roads on STADEN—ROULERS and HOOGLEDE—WESTROOSEBEKE road. Neither of these squadrons met the enemy. Brigade joined up with a FRENCH Cavalry Division and became slightly engaged at Pt. 29. Regiment did not take part in this engagement. Billeted at 6 p.m. N. of Pt. 29.

1st LIFE GUARDS

N. of Pt. 29—Oct. 19, 6 A.M.—Brigade marched in accordance with—

B.M. 2.

To 1st Life Guards, K. Battery.
2nd Life Guards, Field Amb.

1.—Units will assemble with 1st Echelon Transport at Brigade Headquarters (Pt. 29) at 6 a.m.

2.—Commanding Officers will come to Brigade Headquarters at 6 a.m.

3.—2nd Echelon Transport will be drawn up on the road to PASSCHENDEALE at 8 a.m. The leading vehicle will be at the Cross Roads 1 mile S. of the B. of WESTROOSEBEKE. Order of march :—

2nd Life Guards.
Royal Horse Artillery.
Ambulance.
1st Life Guards.
Blues.

It will march to PASSCHENDEALE and halt there. No vehicle will be on the road before 7 a.m.

N. NEILL, Captain,
Brigade-Major, 7th Cavalry Brigade.

5 a.m., *October 19th, 1914.*

to 11th kilometre stone on ROULERS—MENIN road. On arrival there it became heavily engaged with hostile infantry and artillery. Maintained position for three hours ; and then retired on MOORSLEDE. Heavy casualties in 2nd Life Guards Regiment. Lost Lt. Sir P. BROCKLEHURST wounded and one man killed and 4 wounded. 6th Cavalry Brigade practically not engaged. 7th Division also forced to retire in front of superior numbers. FRENCH Cavalry Division acted on our left.

1st LIFE GUARDS.
CASUALTY LIST, OCTOBER 19, 1914.

Killed.—No. 6253 Private A. Stone.   *Wounded.*—Lieutenant Sir Philip Brocklehurst, No. 6427 Private P. Keane, No. 2954 Trooper H. Banks, No. 8713 Private W. Renton, No. 5251 Corporal J. Pocklington, No. 5204 Private W. Sweetman (broken leg).

ROULERS reported in flames. Retired behind FRENCH Division of 10th Corps to ZONNEBEKE and billeted.

Zonnebeke—Oct. 19, 12 MIDNIGHT.—Lt.-Col. H.H. Duke of TECK, G.C.B., etc., returned to the base sick. Major E. H. BRASSEY, M.V.O., took over temporary command of the Regiment.

Zonnebeke—Oct. 20, 5.30 A.M.—Regiment marched to take up a line on right of Brigade, with left resting on railway crossing on ZONNEBEKE—PASSCHENDEALE road. On arrival this line was entrenched and communication was opened with 7th Division on our right.

OPERATION ORDER 7th CAVALRY BRIGADE.

1.—The Brigade will take up a defensive position from ZONNEBEKE (exclusive) to Cross Roads N.E. of ST. JULIEN (inclusive). The 6th Cavalry Brigade is prolonging this line to LANGEMARK.

2.—The 1st Life Guards will occupy the line from ZONNEBEKE (exclusive) to Road Junction N. of K. in ZONNEBEKE (inclusive).

The Royal Horse Guards from Road Junction N. of K. in ZONNEBEKE (exclusive) to Cross Roads S. of E. in HANNEBECK (inclusive).

The 2nd Life Guards from Cross Roads S. of E. in HANNEBECK (exclusive) to Cross Roads N.E. of ST. JULIEN (inclusive).

3.—Reports to Road Junction N. of K. in ZONNEBEKE.

October 20th, 2.4 a.m.   C. M. KAVANAGH, Brig.-General.

WAR DIARY OF

At 10 a.m. Orders were received to hold on to this line as long as possible as 1st Corps was expected at 1 p.m. A battalion of FRENCH 79th Territorial Regiment which retired through the position was intercepted and asked to support the Regiment, this they did. The enemy did not advance nearer than 1,500 yards from the position, but at 12.30 p.m. the town of PASSCHENDEALE which had been held by a FRENCH Cavalry Division, fell into the hands of the enemy and the Regiment was forced to retire on ST. JULIEN, where the Brigade had been ordered to concentrate on retirement. List of casualties all caused by shrapnel.

1st LIFE GUARDS.
CASUALTY LIST, OCTOBER 20TH, 1914.

Wounded.—C. of H., E. Oram, W. Bishop, Private J. Yalden, 2608 W. C. Marsh.
Killed.—No. 6108 Corporal W. Rhodes.

A night attack on ZONNEBEKE prevented the Brigade from returning to billets there as had been intended. At 10 p.m. Brigade went into billets at FREZENBERG. With reference to SL. 42 22nd Brigade, this gap was filled by 2 troops of A Squadron under Major Sir F. CARDEN.

Captain A. H. KEARSEY 10th R. Hussars attached 1st Life Guards took over duties of B.M. 7th Cavalry Brigade.

SL. 42.
To 1st Life Guards.

"There is at present a gap between the right of your line and my left. I am arranging to protect this gap temporarily, but will you please detail troops to fill it and to carry on work being executed as early as possible."

From 22nd Brigade, Zonnebeke, 8.45 a.m.   R. V. BAILEY, Captain.

B.R.2.
To 1st Life Guards, South of PASSCHENDEALE.

"If forced to retire keep in touch with flank of 7th Division, falling back to position N.W. of ZONNEBEKE on line of ZONNEBEKE—LANGEMARK road. The 1st Corps is expected about 1 p.m. to-day, so remain where you are if you can."

From 7th Cavalry Brigade, 9.20 a.m.   C. M. KAVANAGH.

To Captain HARDY, 6 N. railway line between ZONNEBEKE and PASSCHENDEALE, 10.50.

"Am in position along railway line on right of and in prolongation of C Squadron. There was still a gap between me and the British Infantry on my right but a Company of FRENCH troops has now filled it. I shall stay here till further orders unless compelled to retire. I have not seen the General of 22nd Infantry Brigade, but Major SHEARMAN 10th Hussars is going to him, and has promised to report that I am here."

Major CARDEN.

To 1st Life Guards.

"Brigade retiring to position ZONNEBEKE—ST. JULIEN, fall back as already ordered."

12.10 p.m.   BRIGADIER-GENERAL.

Frezenberg—Oct. 21, 5.30 A.M.—Brigade marched out to protect right flank of 1st Corps in their advance towards line OOSTNIEWEKERKE—STADEN.

OPERATION ORDERS NO. 13.
By Brigadier-General C. M. KAVANAGH, C.V.O., C.B., D.S.O.,
Commanding 7th Cavalry Brigade.

FREZENBERG,
October 21st, 1914.

1.—The 7th Division will maintain its present position. The 1st Corps is moving forward towards the line OOSTNIEWEKERKE—STADEN at 7 a.m. to-day.

2.—The Cavalry Division will protect the right flank of the 1st Corps during its advance.

3.—The 6th Cavalry Brigade and "C" Battery, Royal Horse Artillery, will be at Road Junction 200 yards West of 5 kilometre on YPRES—MENIN road at 6.30 a.m. The 7th Cavalry Brigade will concentrate at EKSTERNEST at 6 a.m.

1st LIFE GUARDS

4.—The Brigade will march at 6 a.m., starting point Cross Roads at FREZENBERG

5.—Order of March :—
- 1st Life Guards.
- Royal Horse Guards.
- "K" Battery Royal Horse Artillery.
- Detachment Field Squadron.
- 2nd Life Guards.
- Field Ambulance.
- "A" Echelon 1st Line of Transport.

6.—1st Life Guards will have a Squadron at EKSTERNEST by 6 a.m. as advanced guard of the Brigade, and by 6.30 a.m. will have the concentration of the Brigade covered on the East. "A" Echelon 1st Line of Transport will follow in order of march in rear of Brigade under command of Captain NAPER, Royal Horse Guards. "B" Echelon will march under orders of Brigade Transport Officer at 6.30 a.m., starting point Cross Roads FREZENBERG.

7.—Reports to head of main body.

Issued at 5 a.m.

C. M. KAVANAGH, Brigadier-General,
Commanding 7th Cavalry Brigade.

A Squadron acted as A.G. C Squadron as left flank guard to protect concentration of Brigade at EKSTERNEST. At 9 a.m. moved to railway crossing ½ mile S.W. of ZONNEBEKE, at which point right of 1st Corps joined left of 7th Division. Halted till 11 a.m. when Brigade moved into position W. of ZONNEBEKE to support 22nd Brigade. This was held till 3.30 p.m. when Brigade retired to billets at VOORMEZEELE, Regiment billeted at ST. ELOI. This movement was dictated by the possibility of 2nd Cavalry Division requiring support on line WYTSCHAETE—OOSTAVERNE.

Casualty List and Brigade Order referring to action of Brigade at ZONNEBEKE.

1ST LIFE GUARDS.
CASUALTY LIST, OCTOBER 21ST, 1914.

Killed.—Nil. *Wounded.*—No. 2433 C. of H. H. Tapsell.

To 1st Life Guards.

"The Brigadier has much pleasure in telling the Regiments of the Brigade that before he left ZONNEBEKE to-day, General LAWFORD, Commanding the 22nd Brigade, asked him to express to the Regiments of this Brigade his thanks for the assistance they gave him and his admiration for the way they behaved in saving what might have been a critical situation."

From 7th Cavalry Brigade, VOORMEZEELE, 7 p.m.   A. KEARSAY, Captain, Act. B.M.

B.M.5.

To 1st Life Guards.

"Troops of the 2nd Cavalry Division are now at HOLLEBEKE. Please send patrols at 5 a.m. to-morrow to line WYTSCHAETE—OOSTTAVERNE and also to HOLLEBEKE to gain touch with 2nd Cavalry Division."

From 7th Cavalry Brigade, VOORMEZEELE, 7.45 p.m.   A. KEARSEY, Captain.

St. Eloi—Oct. 22, 6.15 A.M.—Brigade moved to HOOGE, where Regiment remained in reserve all day, retiring to billets at 6 p.m. to KLEIN ZILLEBEKE.

THE OFFICER COMMANDING 1st LIFE GUARDS.

WARNING ORDER.

B.M.6.

"The 7th Cavalry Brigade will march to-morrow to HOOGE at 6.15 a.m. The Brigade will march in the following order :—
- 2nd Life Guards.
- Royal Horse Guards.
- K Battery, Royal Horse Artillery.
- 1st Life Guards.

"The Officer Commanding 2nd Life Guards will detail 1 Squadron as advanced guard Starting point is Road Junction, ½ mile N. of first *T* in KRUISSTRAAT."

A. KEARSEY, Captain,
Brigade-Major, 7th Cavalry Brigade.

VOORMEZEELE,
October 21st, 1914.

WAR DIARY OF

Klein Zillebeke—Oct. 23, 8.30 A.M.—Brigade ordered to relieve 6th Cavalry Brigade in trenches on line of ZANDVOORDE—HOLLEBEKE road.

On arrival below position Brigade Staff rode forward with Commanding Officers and Squadron leaders to have position of trenches pointed out to them by 6th Brigade. While standing on crest of position two shells burst over them, and all were hit except 3 squadron leaders of Regiment. Officers of Brigade Staff only had their clothing torn, but Major BRASSEY had his ear grazed, and Lieutenant Marquess of TWEEDDALE had his lips cut by a shrapnel bullet. It was then decided that it was not safe to relieve the trenches before dark, so Brigade returned to KLEIN ZILLEBEKE till dusk, when it again advanced and took over trenches, Regiment on left of line joining 7th Division at ZANDVOORDE.

B.M.19.

To 1st Life Guards.

"The Brigade will assemble at 8.15 a.m. in the following order:—Royal Horse Guards, 1st Life Guards, "K" Battery, and Headquarters, 2nd Life Guards. Starting point Road Junction, 200 yards S.E. of last *E* in KLEIN ZILLEBEKE, wagons for supplies to be sent to ZILLEBEKE to refill and to bring supplies to ZANDVOORDE, then to return to load up baggage and be ready to start, all available men now with Transport and led horses should parade with Units, one man only being left with four led horses."

From 7th Cavalry Brigade, KLEIN ZILLEBEKE.   A. KEARSEY, Captain, Act. B.M.

Zandvoorde—Oct. 24 and 25.—Remained in trenches for forty-eight hours, trenches heavily shelled all day. Both nights heavy firing opened about 9 p.m. but no actual attack was made. Firing lasted about half an hour, and the same was repeated at about 2 a.m. Reports and Casualty List—

1st LIFE GUARDS.
C SQUADRON CASUALTY LIST.

5759	Private	North	*Wounded*	October 24th, 1914.
5787	,,	Harvey	,,	October 25th, 1914.
2876	,,	Hinton	,,	,,
5265	,,	Whitehead	*Killed*	,,

1st LIFE GUARDS.
CASUALTY LIST, OCTOBER 24TH, 1914.

Killed.—Lieutenant Sir Richard Levinge, No. 6078 Private A. Farmer, No. 4964 Private H. McMullan. *Wounded.*—Private T. Byron.

1st LIFE GUARDS.
CASUALTY LIST, OCTOBER 25TH, 1914.

Killed.—No. 2514 Private E. Lawson. *Wounded.*—Lieutenant Sir Richard V. Sutton, No. 2874 Trooper F. Smith, No. 5779 Private R. Smith.

Zandvoorde—Oct. 25, 6 P.M.—Regiment relieved in trenches by 6th Cavalry Brigade. Owing to a confusion among the men told off to guide the reliefs to the trenches, and also to the fact that 6th Brigade had only 2 Regiments with which to relieve 3, C Squadron were not relieved, and had to remain in the trenches for a further 24 hours.

Regiment less C Squadron and M.G. Section returned to billets at KLEIN ZILLEBEKE. M.G. Sections of Brigade remained in reserve to support 6th Brigade.

1st LIFE GUARDS

Klein Zillebeke—Oct. 25, 9 P.M.—The usual firing started in the trenches (see above). A verbal message was received to say 6th Brigade required support. Only H.Q. and A Squadron had up to then arrived in billets. Turned out dismounted, but before moving off order was cancelled. It afterwards transpired that cyclist who brought verbal message from 6th Brigade had mis-interpreted his orders, message should have merely asked Brigade to stand to.

B.M.8.

To 1st Life Guards.

"Information, Oct. 24, 1914.—The 1st Army Corps was attacked last night five times by enemy who advanced in fours brandishing their rifles over their heads singing 'Wacht am Rheim.' The 1st Corps captured 600 and killed about 1,500, who lay in heaps. The enemy are reported as very brave but entirely ignorant of warfare.

"The 2nd Division aided by a Brigade of 1st Army Corps cleared the wood S. of ZONNE-BEKE and re-captured their trenches. The wood is reported full of dead Germans. The BELGIANS are still holding their own.

"General VON REINHARDT Commanding 54th Division, was killed yesterday."

From 7th Cavalry Brigade, ZANDVOORDE, 8.45 a.m.   A. KEARSEY, Captain.

B.M.17.

To 1st Life Guards.

"Following order received from 3rd Cavalry Division :—On handing over outpost line to-night will you please detail 1 Squadron and all machine-guns to act under orders of G.O.C. 6th Cavalry Brigade. The Royal Horse Guards will detail this Squadron and all machine-guns of Brigade will be on duty to-night ; it is suggested that if all is quiet and there are sufficient men available that horses of M.G. detachments be off-saddled till 4 p.m. to-day."

From 7th Cavalry Brigade, ZANDVOORDE, 10.10 a.m.

A. KEARSEY, Captain, Actg. B.M.

B.M.25.

To 1st Life Guards.

"Regiments will arrange for their own protection and alarm posts, in case of an alarm, Regiments will fall in dismounted in the following order :—1st Life Guards, Royal Horse Guards, 2nd Life Guards. Starting point, Road Junction at second *I* of KLEIN ZILLEBEKE. No fires to be lit in the open during darkness, unless orders are received to the contrary. Regiments need not saddle up and stand to arms at dawn."

From 7th Cavalry Brigade, ZANDVOORDE, 7.35 a.m.   A. KEARSEY, Captain, Actg. B.M.

Klein Zillebeke—Oct. 26.—Regiment remained in billets till 2 p.m. At 2 p.m. Regiment marched to carry out attack as per orders.

B.M.21.

To 1st Life Guards.

"The Brigade will march at 2 p.m. in the following order :—Royal Horse Guards. 1st Life Guards, 2nd Life Guards. Starting point, Road Junction at second *I* of KLEIN ZILLEBEKE."

From 7th Cavalry Brigade, KLEIN ZILLEBEKE, 12.48 p.m.

Brigade Orders.

"The 1st Corps is advancing to-day with general objectives BECLEAERE—TERHAND. The 7th Division is also advancing by swinging forward its left, using KRUSEIK as a pivot. The objective of the 3rd Division is KORTEWILDE. The attack will be delivered by the Brigade as follows :—The Royal Horse Guards will advance from the farm ¼ mile N.E. of Chateau at such time as to be level with the Chateau at 3 p.m. They will then advance on KORTEWILDE with the right on the main stream running down the valley. The 1st Life Guards will advance from the Chateau at 3 p.m., their right on the railway, their left on the stream. Machine-gun 1st Life Guards to be on railway. 2nd Life Guards will be in reserve at the Chateau. These attacks will be carried out dismounted, and lead horses will be left near the starting point. Reports to Chateau till 3 p.m., after that to reserve. A Echelon Transport to come to Chateau, B Echelon to remain near present billets. All available entrenching tools to be brought on packs."

On arrival at starting point, order for attack was suspended, and Brigade halted for two hours. At 4.30 p.m. the Royal Horse

Guards made a demonstration towards the Chateau, while the Regiment entrenched a position 400 yards in advance of road junction at second *I* of KLEIN ZILLEBEKE. At 6 p.m. Regiment returned to billets, the line occupied by 3rd Cavalry Division being the first on which 1st Corps and 4th Corps were making their advance on left flank of main line of Allied Army. On right of 3rd Cavalry Division 3rd Cavalry Brigade carried out a successful attack on HOUTHEM.

No. 1.
To 1st Life Guards.

"Private WHITEHEAD was killed last night. There appears to be a considerable force of the enemy to my front and to my right front. They approach to within about seven hundred yards at night. Our shells have not been near them on this flank. Are we to be relieved to-night, should like some rations. The man I sent, Private PRICE, with message to you yesterday has not returned."

From Captain H. GROSVENOR.

Klein Zillebeke—Oct. 26, 10 P.M.—C Squadron returned to billets on being relieved in the trenches by two troops of 2nd Life Guards.

Klein Zillebeke—Oct. 27, 6 A.M.—Regiment saddled up ready to move. At 10 a.m. order to off-saddle received, and Regiment remained in billets.

Klein Zillebeke—Oct. 27, 4.30 P.M.—Regiment paraded to take over trenches from 6th Brigade.

B.M.13.
To 1st Life Guards.

"Regiments will parade as strong as possible, dismounted, in the following order:— Royal Horse Guards, 2nd Life Guards, 1st Life Guards, at 4.30 p.m. Starting point, Road Junction at second *I* of KLEIN ZILLEBEKE. All horses to remain in their present position. A Echelon of first line Transport will be marched to their previous position near the BASSEVILLE River. The Squadron 2nd Life Guards now in the trenches, will be relieved and will remain in the reserve trenches close to Brigade Headquarters."

From 7th Cavalry Brigade, KLEIN ZILLEBEKE, 1.10 p.m. A. KEARSEY, Captain, Actg. B.M.

At 10 p.m. Order received for 2 Troops of Reserve to parade with 1 Squadron 2nd Life Guards to take over trenches from 22nd Infantry Brigade East of ZANDVOORDE. Two Troops of D Squadron detailed for this duty, but on arrival at trenches there was found to be only room for Squadron of 2nd Life Guards.

Zandvoorde—Oct. 28.—Regiment remained all day in trenches.

B.M.2.
To 1st Life Guards.

"Reliable information has again been received that the GERMAN 27th Reserve Corps will attack at 5.30 a.m. KRUSEIK—ZANDVOORDE position."

From Captain A. KEARSEY.

This attack did not extend to front occupied by Regiment.

Zandvoorde—Oct. 29.—Regiment should have been relieved by 6th Brigade at dusk, but during afternoon 6th Brigade were called out to support infantry on left, so Regiment remained in trenches. C Squadron and 2 Troops of D from Reserve relieved 1½ Squadron Royal Horse Guards in trenches.

1st LIFE GUARDS

Zandvoorde—Oct. 30, 6 A.M.—Heavy bombardment of position opened. At 7.30 a.m. position was attacked by large force of infantry. This attack proved successful owing to greatly superior numbers. Regiment retired in good order about 10 a.m. except C Squadron on left flank from which only about ten men got back. Remainder of Squadron missing. Also one machine gun put out of action.

Regiment retired behind 6th Brigade, which turned out to support. 2nd Dragoons and 3rd and 4th Hussars also came to support, but did not come into action. Having gained ZANDVOORDE ridge, enemy did not press the attack very vigorously, and second position occupied by 6th Brigade was not attacked. At dusk this position was taken over by 4th Guards' Brigade.

Verbranden Molen—Oct. 30, 8 P.M.—Regiment billeted.

1st LIFE GUARDS.
CASUALTY LIST, OCTOBER 30TH, 1914.

Killed, S. C. M. Holmes, Sergeant Arthurs, Trooper Sollars, Trooper Buckeridge. *Wounded.*—2nd Lieutenant Lord Althorp, Lance-Corporal Pye, Trooper Bussey, C. of H. Dawes (missing). *Missing.*—Captain Lord Hugh Grosvenor, Captain E. D. F. Kelly, Lieutenant Hon. Gerald Ward, Lieutenant J. Close-Brooks, 100 rank and file."

B.M.18.

To 1st Life Guards.

"Regiments will reform with their horses as soon as possible. When ready report to Brigade Headquarters at Road Junction at first K of KLEIN ZILLEBEKE. All led and spare horses to be sent back to B Echelon-Transport at VERBRANDEN MOLEN."

From 7th Cavalry Brigade, ½ mile N. of ZANDVOORDE.   A. KEARSEY, Captain, B.M.

Verbranden Molen—Oct. 31, 6 A.M.—Regiment moved into woods South of village to wait for orders. At 10 a.m. moved to wood 1 mile South-west of HOOGE and halted. At 1 p.m. orders received from Cavalry Corps to proceed to ST. ELOI to support 3rd Cavalry Brigade. On arrival at ST. ELOI an urgent wire was received recalling Brigade, to support 4th Hussars on line of canal 1 mile South-east of VERBRANDEN MOLEN. Regiment was leading Regiment of Brigade, and on arrival at VERBRANDEN MOLEN moved up to Headquarters of 4th Hussars. At 6 p.m. contradictory orders were received from Generals ALLENBY and BYNG. General ALLENBY ordered 4th Hussars to hand over position to Regiment, General BYNG ordered whole Brigade to billet at VERBRANDEN MOLEN and to be mobile at 6 a.m., November 1st.

Regiment took over position occupied by 2 Squadrons 4th Hussars, of which Regiment one Squadron remained on right of 1st Life Guards.

1st LIFE GUARDS.
CASUALTY LIST, OCTOBER 31ST, 1914.

Killed.—Nil. *Wounded.*—3896 Private Simpson.

1 Mile South-east of Verbranden Molen—Nov. 1st, 6.30 A.M.—Reverse slope of position heavily bombarded by enemy's heavy howitzers. Major BRASSEY wounded in wrist, Captain Hon. A. F. STANLEY took over command of Regiment.

NOTE.—Owing to loss of C Squadron, it should be noted that Regiment worked in 2 Squadrons only from November 1st.

WAR DIARY OF

1st LIFE GUARDS.
Casualty List, November 1st 1914.
Killed.—6282 Private Burrington. *Wounded.*—Major E. H. Brassey, M.V.O., 2052 C. of H. Webb.

B.M.12.

To 1st Life Guards.

"If the French come to relieve you, hand over trenches and retire to last night's billets. Otherwise remain in trenches until relieved and then join Brigade, which is marching at 6 a.m. on Hooge. Your horses will be left in old billets."

From Captain N. Neill, B.M.

At 11 a.m. Regiment relieved by French Infantry, and rejoined Brigade at Hooge.

Message from C. in C. to troops :—

"The German Emperor will arrive in the Field to-day to conduct the operations against the British Army. I call upon all ranks once more to repeat their magnificent effort and show him what British soldiers really are."

B.M.1.

To 1st Life Guards.

"4th Hussars on your right have not been relieved by us but have appealed to their own Commanding Officer for relief. Brigade moves at 6 a.m. to Hooge and will send you instructions later."

From 7th Cavalry Brigade, Verbranden Molen, 5.40 a.m.   N. Neill, Captain, B.M.

Hooge—Nov. 1, 2 p.m.—Brigade moved to Klein Zillebeke to support 4th Guards Brigade.

Regiment remained in reserve. 7 p.m. withdrew to billets at Hooge.

Hooge—Nov. 2, 5.15 a.m.—Brigade moved to a position of readiness in wood 1 mile South of E in Hooge.

B.M.10.

To 1st Life Guards.

"Head of Brigade will pass the White Gate Posts at Eastern End of Hooge village at 5.15 a.m. to-morrow. Starting point will be marked by the lights of the Brigade Motor-car. Order of march :—Blues, 1st, 2nd, Battery, A Echelon. Light Ambulance Wagons will accompany units. Acknowledge."

From 7th Cavalry Brigade, Hooge, 11.40 p.m.   N. Neill, Captain, Brig.-Major.

At 2 p.m. moved to support Infantry before Geluvelt. Came under heavy shell fire while in half-sections on road.

1st LIFE GUARDS.
Casualty List, November 2nd, 1914.
Killed.—Nil. *Wounded.*—Lieutenant C. D. Leyland, 2534 Trooper Morris, 2537 Private Dix, 2174 Private Lightfoot, 2447 Trooper Savage. *Missing.*—6081 Private Coombes.

R.H.G. came into action, but Regiment remained in support. At 6 p.m. retired to billets 1 mile East of Zillebeke.

Zillebeke—Nov. 3, 6 a.m.—Brigade moved to same position of readiness as was occupied previous day. Remained there till 6 p.m. when retired to billets at Verbranden Molen.

Verbranden Molen—Nov. 4, 1 a.m.—Brigade turned out to support 4th (Guards) Brigade. Just as saddling up was completed this order was cancelled, 4th Brigade having successfully repulsed enemy's attack.

1st LIFE GUARDS

Verbranden Molen—Nov. 4, 6 A.M.—Brigade moved to same position of readiness as was occupied previous day.

TO ALL UNITS.

1.—The Head of the Brigade will pass the Road Junction half a mile S.W. of ZILLEBEKE at 6.15 a.m. to-morrow.

Order of march :—
> 2nd Life Guards.
> Blues.
> 1st Life Guards.
> 1st Echelon.
> K Battery.

2.—1st Echelon Wagons will leave billets with their Units, and will halt at the starting point until they fall into their place in Column. Water-carts will accompany 1st Echelon in future.

3.—The Head of the 2nd Echelon in order of march as above, will be at the starting point at 7 a.m.

4.—Light Ambulance Wagons will be with 1st Echelon.

5.—References in Messages and Orders will be made in future to Map of YPRES, Scale $\frac{1}{40000}$ issued herewith.

N. NEILL, Captain,
Brigade-Major, 7th Cavalry Brigade.

VERBRANDEN MOLEN,
November 3rd, 1914.

Its services were not called for during the day, and at 6 p.m. returned to same billets.

Verbranden Molen—Nov. 5, 6 A.M.—The programme of Nov. 4th was repeated again without incident. 5.30 p.m. Brigade retired to same billets. Lieutenant Hon. E. A. FITZROY, Reserve of Officers, 1st Life Guards, and 30 other ranks joined from base.

B.M.1.
To all Units.

"Orders for to-day same as yesterday. Starting point 6.15 a.m. Order of march :— Blues, 1st, 2nd, A Echelon, K Battery. Light Ambulance Wagons with 1st Echelon. 2nd Echelon Transport same as yesterday."

From 7th Cavalry Brigade, VERBRANDEN MOLEN, 4.20 a.m.   N. NEILL, Captain.

Verbranden Molen—Nov. 6, 6 A.M.—Brigade moved to same position as before.

B.M.1.
To 1st and 2nd Life Guards Blues, K. Battery, 7th Cav. F.D., A.M.B.

"General situation remains satisfactory. The Brigade will be in Corps Reserve in same position as yesterday. Head will pass starting point 6.15 a.m. Order of march :— 1st Life Guards, 2nd Life Guards, A Echelon. Blues and K Battery will act in accordance with instructions already issued verbally. Only limbered wagons, water-carts and Light Ambulances will accompany A Echelon. All General Supply Wagons will be with B Echelon."

From 7th Cavalry Brigade, VERBRANDEN MOLEN.   N. NEILL, Captain.

1 Mile S. of E. in Hooge—Nov. 6, 3.15 P.M.—4th (Guards) Brigade asked for support, some FRENCH in occupation of some of the trenches in Brigade Line, having retired and let enemy through ¼ mile E. of ZWARTELEEN.

Regiment dismounted for action ½ mile S. of third *E* in ZILLEBEKE and advanced on road running through first *E* in ZWARTELEEN. 2nd Life Guards were on right and R.H.G. in support. Irish Guards on left. Regiment advanced with D Squadron on left, 2 Troops of A Squadron on right, and 2 Troops A Squadron in support. M.G. Section remained in reserve, the wooded nature of the country not lending itself to the successful employment of Machine Guns in the advance. The advance was successfully carried out on left across open to within 150 yards of wood through first E in ZWARTELEEN. The right did not advance quite so far.

Great difficulty was experienced by all units in keeping touch with Troops on either flank. This was due to thickly-wooded nature of the country. D Squadron were finally forced to retire to South edge of woods by Machine-gun fire.

At dusk 3rd Infantry Brigade arrived to relieve Brigade on this line. Gloucester Regiment detailed for section occupied by 1st Life Guards and 2nd Life Guards. They however proved too weak to take over more than section occupied by 2nd Life Guards. Regiment remained in occupation of line till relieved at 2.30 a.m. by 2 Companies Royal Sussex Regiment, 2 Companies Royal Munster Fusiliers and a few details of Irish Guards.

No. 1.
To 7th Cavalry Brigade.
" A Squadron supported by FRENCH and 2nd Life Guards are advancing and intend taking village at point of bayonet. D Squadron are in touch with Grenadiers on left and are not seriously opposed on front. They are endeavouring to get touch on right where there seems to be a gap. GERMAN shells have begun bursting over wood, so think they are retiring."
From 1st Life Guards, KLEIN ZILLEBEKE, 4.10 P.M.   E. H. WYNDHAM, Capt.

To 1st Life Guards.
" Your line is to be taken over by Worcesters from direction of Irish Guards Headquarters. Try to connect with them and report here. When Worcesters have taken over your line retire on your lead horses and return to place of yesterday's Brigade Headquarters."
From 7th Cavalry Brigade, 12 Midnight, *Nov.* 6.   C. M. KAVANAGH, Brigadier-General.

1st LIFE GUARDS.
CASUALTY LIST, NOVEMBER 6TH, 1914.
Killed.—6656 Corporal Hopkins, 8345 Private Lane, 6785 Private George, 6361 Private Tingley, Lieutenant Hon. W. R. Wyndham. *Wounded.*—Captain L. H. Hardy, Lieutenant Hon. H. W. C. Denison, 2158 S. C. M. Ratcliffe, Lieutenant Hon. E. A. Fitzroy, 5978 Private Henry, 6032 Private Ferrie, 6152 Private Barnes, 6203 Private Childs, 5241 Private Sayers, 5985 Private Wiltcher, 5382 Private Percy, 2798 C. of H., Fleming, 2474 Corporal George, 6010 Corporal Reed, 6642 Private Gilchrist, 5295 Private Murday, 2575 C. of H. Wright, 5821 Sergeant Fraser, 2443 Trooper Scott, 6265 Private McDonald, 2216 Trooper Pearson.

Quarter Mile N. of Second R in Verbranden Molen—Nov. 7, 3.45 A.M.—Regiment rejoined Brigade and bivouacked. 5.30 a.m. Brigade moved to position of readiness to support Infantry attack to recover ground lost previous day at KLEIN ZILLEBEKE. Regiment permitted to remain in bivouac ready to move, in view of late return from firing line. At 8 a.m. Brigade returned to bivouac, Infantry attack having proved successful. Messages from 1st Corps and C. in C. received.

B.R.7.
To 1st Life Guards.
" Keep your Regiment in its present position ready to move when ordered, but as much separated and under cover as possible to avoid loss from shell-fire. Remainder of Brigade will probably return to you before long."
From 7th Cavalry Brigade, 7.45 a.m.   C. M. KAVANAGH, Brig.-General.

To O.C. 1st Life Guards.
" The Brigade will march to-day at 5.30 a.m. Starting point, Road Junction, S.W ZILLEBEKE. Order of march :—
    2nd Life Guards.
    Royal Horse Guards.
    1st Life Guards.
    K Battery Royal Horse Artillery."
    C. M. KAVANAGH, Brig -General.

1st LIFE GUARDS

The following messages are forwarded with the G.O.C.'s congratulations.

1.—From Sir Douglas Haig to G.O.C. 3rd Cavalry Division, November 6th, 1914, 8.25 p.m., begins—

"Sir Douglas Haig wishes to thank General Kavanagh's Brigade for the splendid support given to the Infantry to-day at a very critical moment." (Ends.)

2.—From C. in C. to G.O.C. 1st Army Corps, November 6th, 1914, 11.36 p.m., begins—

"Please thank Cavan and Kavanagh on my behalf for the help they have given to the French. I am making very strong representations to Foch on the subject" (Ends)—Sir Douglas adds that he deeply regrets the heavy loss incurred.

"The Brigadier when forwarding the attached message from the 3rd Cavalry Division, wishes to express his sincere gratitude to the Officers, N.C.O.'s and men of the Brigade for the splendid way they behaved yesterday under very trying circumstances. He would like these messages to be read out to all ranks."
To 1st Life Guards.

Quarter Mile N. of Second R in Verbranden Molen—Nov. 7, 2 P.M.—Brigade moved to billets round VERLOREN HOEK.

Verloren Hoek—Nov. 8.—Brigade remained in billets all day. Captain Hon. C. C. FELLOWES, Reserve of Officers 1st Life Guards, and Lieutenant G. HALSWELL, Reserve of Officers 13th Hussars, and 30 other ranks joined from the base.

Verloren Hoek—Nov. 9, 4.30 P.M.—Regiment found 150 men for trenches at ZWARTELEEN to relieve 3rd D.G.'s.

Verloren Hoek—Nov. 10, 10.30 P.M.—Above party returned to billets having been relieved by 1st Royal Dragoons, in trenches.

CASUALTY LIST, NOVEMBER 10TH, 1914.
Killed.—Nil. *Wounded.*—6251 Private Martin, 2747 Trooper Bomford, 4661 Private Davenport, 764 Private Buckle, 5911 Private Lightfoot.

Verloren Hoek—Nov. 11, 11 A.M.—Brigade turned out to support line E. of HOOGE, which was reported to have been pierced by enemy. Services of Brigade were however not required, and at 2.30 p.m. returned to billets. Lieutenant Lord SOMERS returned to base sick.

Verloren Hoek—Nov. 11, 3 P.M.—H.Q. and 1st Life Guards' Squadron belonging to Composite Regiment of Household Cavalry hitherto forming part of 4th Cavalry Brigade, joined Regiment on absorption.

B.M.4.
To 1st Life Guards.
"Notice has been received from Cavalry Corps, that the Composite Household Cavalry Regiment will arrive to-day and will at once be sent to their Regiments. Each Squadron will join its own Regiment."
From Captain A KEARSEY.

Composite Squadron in future numbered B Squadron.

Verloren Hoek—Nov. 11, 5 P.M.—Brigade turned out and moved to position of readiness S. of BELLEWARDE FARM to support counter-attack by 1st Division to regain line of trenches lost earlier in afternoon from S.W. corner of POLYGONE DE ZONNEBEKE to V. in VELDHOEK. 10 p.m.—Brigade returned to billets with orders to be ready to move at any moment during the night.

WAR DIARY OF

Verloren Hoek—Nov. 12, 1 A.M.—Regiment turned out dismounted and proceeded to HOOGE to receive orders from G.O.C. 1st Division.

B.M.3.

To 1st Life Guards.

"The Regiment will move at once without horses to kilometre 4 on MENIN road."

From 7th Cavalry Brigade, 1.35 a.m.

Remainder of Brigade ordered to turn out mounted at 4 a.m. and rendezvous at same place.

Hooge—Nov. 12, 4 A.M.—In accordance with verbal orders received from G.O.C. 1st Division D Squadron occupied line of reserve trenches E. of HOOGE CHATEAU. Remaining 2 Squadrons were ordered to extend behind trenches occupied by Gloucesters along W. edge of square K15 to be ready to support counter-attack from S.W. corner of POLYGONE DE ZONNEBEKE. On arrival on this line C.O. reported to G.O.C. 1st Infantry Brigade at VERBEEK FARM, who recommended that the 2 Squadrons should be moved into dug-outs at S.E. corner of NONNE BOSSCHEN, as if they remained in their present exposed position they would probably suffer very heavily from shell fire. This move was carried out just before dawn, and D Squadron also moved up to same dug-outs. 1st Brigade then retired on HOOGE. At noon Regiment was relieved by Queen's Bays and returned to billets.

CASUALTY LIST, NOVEMBER 12TH, 1914.

Killed.—Nil.   *Wounded.*—6150 Lance-Corporal Evans, 5986 Private Warren.

Verloren Hoek—Nov. 13.—Capt. Hon. C. C. FELLOWES returned to base sick. Captain and Quarter-Master W. GARTON returned to base having been relieved by Captain and Quartermaster C. YEATMAN, 1st Life Guards. Reliefs for trenches supplied in accordance with B.M. 16:—

B.M.16.

To 1st Life Guards.

" Reference B.M. 13, Royal Horse Guards, will find 380 rifles and 1st Life Guards 120 rifles to relieve trenches of 6th Cavalry Brigade. They will parade under Major the Lord Tweedmouth at 4.15 p.m. at starting point at railway crossing S.W. of 2nd Life Guards' billets. They will be dismounted, they will be marched under Lord Tweedmouth to vicinity of KLEIN ZILLEBEKE."

From 7th Cavalry Brigade, 12.50 P.M.   A. KEARSEY, Captain.

Expected attack mentioned in B.M.14 did not develop and Brigade did not have to turn out.

B.M.14.

To 1st Life Guards.

" French on CAVAN's right being shelled. In view of the information from two sources that Germans intend to-day to press in at this point, please keep ready to move at a moment's notice. Order of march :—
    Royal Horse Guards.
    1st Life Guards.
    Leicestershire Yeomanry.

" Starting point, railway crossing S.W. 2nd Life Guards' billets. Hour of start—notified later."

From Captain A. KEARSEY.

Verloren Hoek—Nov. 14, 5 P.M.—Reliefs of trenches carried out in accordance with B.M. 19.

1st LIFE GUARDS

B.M.19.

To 1st Life Guards.

"The following reliefs will be carried out to-night. 1st Life Guards 260 rifles and 2nd Life Guards 40 rifles and Machine-gun will occupy the front trenches. 200 rifles of the 2nd Life Guards will occupy the supporting trenches. In the Reserve trenches there will be 140 rifles of the 2nd Life Guards and 160 rifles of the Leicestershire Yeomanry. The front and supporting trenches will be under the command of Major The Hon. A. Stanley. Reserve trenches will be under command of Senior Officer with 2nd Life Guards. Starting point railway crossing S.W. 2nd Life Guards' billets at 5 p.m."

From 7th Cavalry Brigade, 1.30 p.m.   A. KEARSEY, Captain.

B Squadron and 1 Troop A were relieved from support trenches.

Zwarteleen—Nov. 15.—In trenches all day. Position was shelled with high explosive shells for 1½ hours in morning. No damage was done. About 3 p.m. 2nd Lieutenant H. B. ST. GEORGE came to Headquarters from advanced trenches, and reported that enemy seemed to have evacuated advanced trenches at edge of wood at Z in ZWARTELEEN. This was thought to be due to the very heavy shell fire which had been brought to bear on these trenches by one of our batteries in position somewhere about N. edge of square K.17 C. On setting out to return to trenches 2nd Lieutenant ST. GEORGE was shot dead by a sniper apparently posted in a house on ZILLEBEKE—KLEIN ZILLEBEKE road. Other casualties, as per list, all caused by snipers.

CASUALTY LIST, NOVEMBER 15TH, 1914.

Killed.—2nd Lieutenant H. A. B. St. George. *Wounded.*—2513 C. of H., Haywood 5454 Sergeant Roantree.

At 7 p.m. Regiment was relieved by 3rd D.G.'s and N. Somerset I.Y., and returned to billets at VERLOREN HOEK.

Verloren Hoek—Nov. 16.—The Regiment remained in billets. At 5 p.m. 350 rifles marched out as ordered in B.R. 25.

B.R.25.

To 1st Life Guards.

"The 400 men of 7th Cavalry Brigade now forming 1st Corps Reserve will be relieved at 5 p.m. to-night by the following :—

1st Life Guards 350.
2nd Life Guards 50.

The whole under the command of Major Hon. A. STANLEY, 1st Life Guards. They will march in above order at 4.30 p.m. Starting point railway crossing S.W. 2nd Life Guards' billets. They will be situated as follows :—

"In Dug-outs, near Railway Bridge S.W. of HALTE, 150 1st Life Guards. In farm lately occupied by Headquarters, 6th Cavalry Brigade, 200 1st Life Guards, 50 2nd Life Guards. Headquarters with latter party."

From C. M. KAVANAGH, Brigadier-General.

B.R. 28.

To Major STANLEY, 1st Life Guards.

"The 400 men under your command will not be required as a Reserve after 8 a.m. to-morrow morning. At that hour they can march back to their billets."

From 7th Cavalry Brigade.   C. M. KAVANAGH, Brig.-General.

Verloren Hoek—Nov. 17.—Regiment remained in billets till 12.30 p.m.

At 12.30 p.m. marched in accordance with B.M.8 to BEGERSBURG (J.2. a).

WAR DIARY OF

B.M.8.

To 1st Life Guards.

The Brigade will march at 12.30 p.m. in the following order :—
    2nd Life Guards.
    Royal Horse Guards.
    1st Life Guards.
    A Echelon Transport.
    B Echelon Transport.

Starting point, Road Junction, ¾ mile N. of Royal Horse Guards' billets.

From 7th Cavalry Brigade, 11.25.   A. KEARSEY, Captain.

Rifles for trenches as per B.M.1 were ordered to parade mounted as soon as billets at BEGERSBURG had been occupied.

B.M.1.

To 1st Life Guards.

Following will be required for the trenches to-night :—

2nd Life Guards	310 rifles and machine-guns.
1st Life Guards	310 ,, ,, ,,
Royal Horse Guards	310 ,, ,, ,,
Leicestershire Yeomanry	240 ,, ,, ,,

From 7th Cavalry Brigade, 8.15 a.m.   A. KEARSEY, Captain.

Just as Brigade was parading, order was changed, and rifles found by 1st Life Guards, marched dismounted to dug-outs occupied during night of 16th-17th to act as Corps Reserve.

B.M.

To 1st Life Guards.

The following is the detail of the trenches for forty-eight hours, commencing 6 p.m. to-night :—

Right Section (Captain TORRIE, 2nd Life Guards).

Advanced Trenches 280 2nd Life Guards and Machine-guns in addition.

Support Trench (*a*) 30 2nd Life Guards.
                50 1st Life Guards.
        (*b*) 120 1st Life Guards.

Reserve near Lord Cavan's Headquarters :—
    140 1st Life Guards   ⎫ Under Senior Officer
    60 Leicester Yeomanry ⎬ 1st Life Guards.

Left Section (Major Lord TWEEDMOUTH, Royal Horse Guards).

Advanced Trenches 310 Royal Horse Guards.
                  80 Leicester Yeomanry and Machine-guns.

Support Trenches   100 Leicester Yeomanry.

From A. KEARSEY, Captain.

Dug-outs in Railway Cutting in J.10.d.—Nov. 18.—Regiment remained in Corps Reserve. D Squadron in farm at *C* in CHEMIN.

Dug-outs in Railway Cutting in J.10.d.—Nov. 19.—Brigade found rifles for trenches as per B.R. 43.

B.R.43.

To 1st Life Guards.

The trenches will be occupied to-night as follows :—

Advanced Trenches.   KLEIN ZILLEBEKE.   100 Leicester Yeomanry and Machine-guns.
                                                             180 1st Life Guards.

Support Trenches.   KLEIN ZILLEBEKE.   80 Leicester Yeomanry.
                                                             120 1st Life Guards.

All under command Major Hon. A. Stanley, 1st Life Guards.

The above to be at ZILLEBEKE Church at 6 p.m.

Lord Cavan's Reserve. Farm N. of ZILLEBEKE.
    Remainder of Leicester Yeomanry.
    150 Royal Horse Guards.
    Under command of Major Brassey, Royal Horse Guards.

1st LIFE GUARDS

General Reserve, near HALTE.
  Remainder Royal Horse Guards.
  2nd Life Guards.
  Under command Major Lord Tweedmouth, Royal Horse Guards.

"The trenches will be occupied as above until night of 20th. Please arrange for supplies and ammunition accordingly. Copies of above are being sent to Headquarters of Regiments in Billeting Areas."

From 7th Cavalry Brigade.   C. M. KAVANAGH, Brig-.General.

Regiment marched to trenches from dug-outs at 5 p.m.

Zartelween—Nov. 20.—Advanced trenches were shelled both morning and afternoon and sufficient damage was done to necessitate the evacuation of those on right under command of Captain HAMILTON STUBBER. On each of the two occasions during the day on which this section were forced to leave the trenches, they took shelter in the trenches occupied by 2nd Battalion 142nd French Infantry, S. of ZILLEBEKE—KLEIN ZILLEBEKE road. On both occasions they re-occupied the damaged trenches at the conclusion of the bombardment.

B.M.6.

To Major the Hon. A. STANLEY.

"Gap in your Line must be swept by cross-fire and supporting trench in rear specially warned to keep sharp look-out. Every effort must be made to remake the trenches at dark before arrival of the French relief. Should this be impossible, supporting trench must be line for French to take over. Am trying to arrange with Cavalry Division for Field Squadron to help with this work."

From 7th Cavalry Brigade, Railway Bridge W. of Halte, 10.35 a.m. A. KEARSEY, Captain.

No movement on the part of the enemy was observed during the day.

1st LIFE GUARDS.
CASUALTY LIST, NOVEMBER 20TH, 1914.

Killed.—2569 C. of H. J. Rose, 6110 Private Hudson, 5991 Private G. Ingram, 8604 Private B. T. Reddington, 2871 Trooper S. Browne, 6171 Private Sinclair, 2920 Trooper Hickling, 2959 Trooper Spoor, 2922 Trooper Helliwell. *Wounded.*—5384 Private J. Smith, 4339 Private Fenton, 5406 Private A. Stewart, 8394 Private Vassie, 1888 Trooper C. Coomer, 5823 Private R. Mitchell, 6866 Private J. Robinson, 5983 Private R. Knott, 2869 Trooper Grays, 2971 Trooper F. Adams, 4946 Private K. Wood, 5347 Private Stewart, 1972 C. of H., P. Bruce, 976 Private F. Russell, 2797 Trooper F. Baxter. *Missing.*—5505 Private S. Tait, 694 Private D. Irwin, 5453 Private S. Dowds.

Zartelween—Nov. 20, 8 P.M.—Brigade was relieved in trenches by a Battalion of 142nd French Infantry. Regiment returned to billets.

B.R.49.

To 1st Life Guards.

"The Troops in trenches may return to billets when relieved by French, about 8.30 p.m. Please tell Colonel Freke that his party with Major Brassey return at 5 p.m. to billets. No wheels allowed on roads, so limbered wagons for ammunition will not come for surplus ammunition."

From 7th Cavalry Brigade.   C. M. KAVANAGH, Brigadier-General.

B.R.47.

To 1st Life Guards.

1.—The Brigade will march to their new billeting area at 9 a.m. to-morrow as follows:—
Starting point Cross Roads, S. of Railway on YPRES—VLAMERTINGE road, one mile West of YPRES:—

      Royal Horse Guards.
      2nd Life Guards.
      Leicestershire Yeomanry.
      1st Life Guards.

2.—" A " Echelon, 1st Line Transport will follow the Brigade in order of march.

WAR DIARY OF

3.—" B " Echelon will march in above order at 8 a.m., under command Captain Molyneux. Starting point, Cross Roads as above.

4.—Route across DICKEBUSH BEEK, VON GROENEN JAGER, OUDERDOM, RENNINGHELST, WESTOUTRE.

5.—K Battery, Royal Horse Artillery, will march independently to the Divisional billeting area.

6.—On arrival at WESTOUTRE, Regiments will march independently to their new billeting areas.

7.—Reports to Head of Column as far as WESTOUTRE, later to new Brigade Headquarters at THIEUSHOEK.

From 7th Cavalry Brigade.   C. M. KAVANAGH, Brigadier-General.

Brigade marched to new billeting area to rest and re-fit.

B.M.10.

To 1st Life Guards.

" The Table of Billeting Areas is forwarded for information. Regimental billeting parties will meet the Staff-Captain mounted at Brigade Headquarters at 7 a.m.

" Billeting Areas, 1st Life Guards Headquarters, MT. DES CATS Monastery, Line S. of GODESWAERVELDE (exclusive) to pt. 75, thence to BERTHEN (exclusive), thence to GODESWAERVELDE. (Ref. Map, $\frac{1}{100000}$).

" 2nd Life Guards Headquarters, near THIEUSHOEK Line from Road Junction N.N.W. of K in KRUISTRAET to CAESTRE (exclusive), thence to FLETRE (exclusive), thence to Road Junction, N.N.W. of K in KRUISTRAET.

" Leicestershire Yeomanry Headquarters, LE COQ DE PAILLE, East of Road FLETRE (exclusive) to pt. 75, thence to BERTHEM (exclusive), thence FONTAINE HOEK (exclusive), thence to FLETRE.

" Brigade Headquarters and Signal Troop, THIEUSHOEK."

From 7th Cavalry Brigade, Railway Bridge, W. of Halte.   A. KEARSEY, Captain.

Bogersburg—Nov. 21, 9 A.M.

On arrival at WESTOUTRE, after a march considerably delayed by crowded state of roads, orders were received that Brigade billeting area had been changed. Regiment finally billeted at 9 p.m. at LA KREULE and in surrounding farms.

La Kreule—Nov. 22—B.R. 57.

B.R.57.

To 1st Life Guards.

" The following extract from a letter from Lord Cavan, Commanding 4th Brigade, is forwarded for your information. Begins :—I must send you and your great Brigade a word of true thanks for having helped so splendidly to maintain my section of the Line.

" I told Sir D. Haig and he will tell Sir John French to-morrow, that I want no finer troops than yours." (Ends.)

From 7th Cavalry Brigade.   C. M. KAVANAGH, Brigadier-General.

La Kreule—Nov. 23.—H.R.H. The Prince of Wales visited the Regiment.

La Kreule—Dec. 1.—The under-mentioned awards to Officers, N.C.O.'s and men of Regiment published—

D.S.O.—Major Hon. A. F. STANLEY.
D.C.M.—2798 C. of H. J. FLEMING.
3043 C. of H. J. BAILLIE.
2399 Corporal E. BEACH.
2653 Trooper R. LEWIS.

Capt. J. J. ASTOR, 1st Life Guards, joined for duty on recovery from wounds, and took command of D Squadron.

1st LIFE GUARDS

la Kreule—Dec. 2.—H.M. The KING inspected 3rd Cavalry Division at HAZEBROUCK.

Ebblinghem—Dec. 7.—Regiment moved to billets round EBBLINGHEM.

Officers joined :—

Major L. E. Barry	December 3rd, 1914	} 6 men.
Lieutenant G. H. Preston	,, ,, ,,	
,, G. C. Bostock	,, ,, ,,	
,, E. R. Hoare	,, 6th, ,,	
,, G. C. Barker	,, ,, ,,	
,, M. Seton Karr	,, ,, ,,	} 27 men.
,, J. S. Woolley	,, ,, ,,	
,, L. P. Payne Gallwey	,, ,, ,,	
,, T. Nottidge	,, ,, ,,	

Dec. 13.

B.M.3.

To 1st Life Guards.

"The Brigade will march to-morrow at 7.0 a.m. Starting point, Cross Roads, South of *D* in HONDEGHEM. Order of march :—1st Life Guards to move to starting point, *via* LE HEYL and LE CHATEAU, 2nd Life Guards, Leicestershire Yeomanry. A Echelon will follow fighting troops in order of march. B Echelon will march at 10 a.m. from same starting point in order of march, and on reaching FLETRE will be conducted to billets by their billeting parties. 7th Cavalry Brigade Field Ambulance will march in rear of B Echelon, the Officer Commanding sending Motor Ambulance to be at WESTOUTRE at 10 a.m."

From 7th Cavalry Brigade.   C. M. KAVANAGH, Brigadier-General.

Ebblinghem—Dec. 14.—Brigade marched in accordance with B.M.3 to act as mobile reserve to 2nd Corps who were taking offensive about WYTSCHAETE.

Brigade waited in position of readiness at SCHERPENBERG till 2 p.m., at which hour G.O.C. 2nd Corps was able to dispense with its services owing to the success of the Infantry attack. Regiment billeted at BERTHEN.

B.M.5.

To 1st Life Guards, repeated to 2nd Life Guards, Leicestershire Yeomanry, Brigade Supply Officer and 7th Cavalry Field Ambulance.

"Brigade will not saddle up to-morrow without further orders, but will be ready to move at half-an-hour's notice. Saddles to be ready packed close to horses. A Echelon vehicles to remain packed."

From 7th Cavalry Brigade.

Berthen—Dec. 15.—Brigade remained in billets.

Ebblinghem—Dec. 16.—Brigade returned to former billets. Regiment remained at EBBLINGHEM for remainder of December.

Major A. M. PIRIE, D.S.O., Reserve of Officers, 21st Lancers, joined as 2nd in Command.

Jan. 1915.—Throughout the month of January the Regiment remained in billets about EBBLINGHEM and WALLONCAPELLE, without being called upon to take part in any active operations at the front. Various squadron, regimental, and brigade exercises were carried out during this period, and reserve machine-gunners were trained. A party of 10 men were also chosen to be exercised as snipers under

WAR DIARY OF

Lieutenant C. WATERHOUSE. Lieutenant W. R. PORTAL joined from the Base during the month, and was posted to A Squadron. Four other ranks also joined.

Jan. 27.—The Field-Marshal Commanding-in-Chief inspected the Regiment.

The Field-Marshal addressed the troops as follows:—

1st Life Guards.

"It gives me great pleasure on this the first opportunity available to thank all ranks for the exceptional way you have behaved in this campaign.

"You have upheld and added to the glorious traditions of your famous Regiment, and acquitted yourselves as all who knew the 1st Life Guards would have expected.

"It was through the masterly way in which you were led by General Byng (Commanding 3rd Cavalry Division) and your Brigadier, Brigadier-General Kavanagh (Commanding 7th Cavalry Brigade), that we are able to hold and maintain the positions we occupy to-day.

"But there is one thing it grieves me to speak about and that is we have to mourn the loss of so many of your brave comrades. Your ranks have been sadly depleted. I feel I must mention the loss of your brave Colonel, Colonel Cook, who died from his wounds.

"It is not the first time that I have had the pleasure of being associated with the 1st Life Guards, for I well remember your magnificent Squadron in South Africa, so ably led by Colonel Carter, more especially at Colesburg and Kimberley.

"Again I thank all Officers, Non-Commissioned Officers and Troopers for their gallant behaviour and trust that by our united efforts we shall bring the war to a swift and speedy termination."

Ebblinghem—Feb. 1.—Nothing to report on February 1 and 2.

Feb. 3, 2 p.m.—3rd Cavalry Division having been ordered to take over a section of the line E. of YPRES from the French, the Regiment proceeded by motor-bus in accordance with Orders:—

REGIMENTAL ORDERS BY MAJOR THE HON. A. F. STANLEY, D.S.O.,
COMMANDING 1st LIFE GUARDS.

"Orders for taking over the trenches on the night February 3rd-4th by the 7th Cavalry Brigade and part of 8th Cavalry Brigade.

"The following will be the procedure for taking over the trenches East of YPRES to-morrow, by 7th Cavalry Brigade and four Squadrons 8th Cavalry Brigade.

"The troops will be conveyed in motor-buses to the corner of the HOOGE road, East of YPRES."

"They will, after dismounting, then fall in in the following order:—

2nd Life Guards.
Leicester Yeomanry.   } 7th Cavalry Brigade.
1st Life Guards
1 Squadron Essex Yeomanry. } 8th Cavalry Brigade.
Royal Horse Guards.

"Order of march:—
D.
B.
A.
M.G.

"The limbered wagons carrying the machine-guns of each regiment will fall in in rear of their respective regiments. The remainder of the A Echelon transport, drawn up in the order of march on the HOOGE road, will remain halted.

"About 6 p.m. Regiments will march off at intervals of ten minutes via HALTE and ZILLEBEKE to Lord Cavan's Headquarters, with guides who will join them at the starting-point.

"On arrival at Lord Cavan's Headquarters, units of the 7th Cavalry Brigade will branch off and concentrate in rear of the support trenches on the right of the line, and on arrival there will start taking over the trenches from the French, starting from the right.

1st LIFE GUARDS

"Units of the 8th Cavalry Brigade, under command of Major Lord Tweedmouth, Royal Horse Guards, will march to the support trenches on the left of the line and take over the trenches from the French, starting from the right of the portion of the line allotted to them.

"All units before leaving Lord Cavan's house will take their machine-guns from the limbers and carry them the remainder of the way.

"The empty limbers will then return viâ ZILLEBEKE and HALTE to YPRES.

"On arrival at Lord Cavan's Headquarters the Officer Commanding 2nd Life Guards will detail a guard to take charge of the baggage and ammunition of the units of the 7th Cavalry Brigade, which will be unloaded there during the night, and the Officer Commanding Royal Horse Guards will detail a similar guard for the baggage of the units of the 8th Cavalry Brigade.

"When it is considered safe to do so, the Officer Commanding A Echelon 7th Cavalry Brigade, will send off the remainder of the vehicles of his Echelon in batches of four vehicles at a time viâ HALTE and ZILLEBEKE to Lord Cavan's house, where they will be met by a Staff Officer, 7th Cavalry Brigade, and fatigue parties from the reserve Squadrons 7th and 8th Cavalry Brigades, and unloaded by them.

"The vehicles will then return to YPRES by the same route, but no vehicles must pass ZILLEBEKE on the outward journey until those on the return journey have got back to that place.

"The fatigue parties above-mentioned will be detailed by Colonel Ferguson, 2nd Life Guards, and Major Lord Tweedmouth, Royal Horse Guards, and these parties, after unloading the baggage, will carry it to the support trenches, where the troops themselves will take it over.

"Rations for Thursday, February 4th, will be brought up to the same point after the baggage has been unloaded, and must also be brought up to the support trenches by the same fatigue parties.

"Water-carts for units will be brought to the same point, and remain there during the night, returning to YPRES before daylight on the 4th.

"Water-bottles and dixies must be filled from these carts by men sent from the trenches for the purpose.

"Besides the two hundred rounds on the man, one box of ammunition per troop and two boxes per machine-gun must be placed in the trenches. The remainder will be left in the support trenches.

"Besides the men posted in the 'listening posts,' one man per section must be alert during the night.

"The rifles of the remainder should be placed in the loopholes, the men sleeping close to them.

"Unless further orders are received, Squadrons and Machine-gun Section will rendezvous at STAPLE at 1.45 p.m., from which place motor-buses will start at 2 p.m."

(Signed) E. H. WYNDHAM, Captain,
Adjutant, 1st Life Guards.

2nd February, 1915.

On arrival at junction of YPRES—ZONNEBEKE and YPRES—MENIN roads, the Regiment left the buses and marched via ZILLEBEKE to take over trenches E. of N.E. end of brown road running N.E. from ZWARTELEEN. The Royal Horse Guards were on the left of the Regiment, and Leicestershire Yeomanry on the right. Beyond the former was a Squadron of Essex Yeomanry and beyond the latter a Squadron of 2nd Life Guards. Fighting strength in trenches 17 officers and 250 rifles. Artillery support was provided by the FRENCH, instructions relating to this support received from G.O.C. 18th FRENCH Division as follows:—

18th Division,
Staff No. 95.   Headquarters, 2nd of February, 1915.

NOTE FOR THE GENERAL COMMANDER OF THE 3RD BRITISH CAVALRY DIVISION.

(LIAISONS WITH THE FRENCH ARTILLERY.)

"The 3rd British Cavalry Division having no Artillery at its disposal, will always be seconded in case of need by the French Artillery.

WAR DIARY OF

"To that effect, a liaison Officer Observer of Artillery is on post near each reports place of the two Superior Officers of the English Cavalry.

"Besides, the latter have a telephone-wire with the French Colonel commanding the sector South of the 18th Division at Hooge.

"The English Superior Officers will, in case of need, ask for the help of Artillery:—

"1° *in day-time*: to the liaison Artillery Officer who is near their reports place.

"2° *in night-time*: by using the telephone with the French Colonel commanding the sector South of the 18th Division at Hooge.

"NOTA.—In day-time, if the wire that joins the Artillery Officer with the batteries is cut off, it would be necessary to apply as in night-time to the Colonel commanding the sector South at Hooge.

"In order that those liaisons may be done under good conditions, it is necessary that the General commanding the 3rd British Cavalry Division should have an interpreter at the two reports places of his two superior Officers, the Colonel commanding the sector South of the French Division having not any.

"The liaison with the Artillery being of capital importance, this understanding must be realised in the night of the 3rd to the 4th of February, and the English Officer must be sure that everything is going right before the chiefs of the French battalions have left."

General LEFEVRE, Commander of the 18th Division.

"NOTA.—Besides, in night-time, if the telephone-wires are broken, the Superior Officer may request from the Artillery the execution of a 'barrage fire,' by means of a cluster of 3 shining rockets shot from his reports place.

"To that effect several rockets will be left next night at the reports places of the two relieved chiefs of battalions.

"The French Infantry will show the way to use them."

9th Corps d'Armée.
18th Division.
Etat-Major Brigade. Bureau.
No. 100.

Headquarters on the 4th of February, 1915.

NOTE OF SERVICE.

"In spite of all the prescriptions of the General Commander of the Division, it happens very often what follows:—

"When our Artillery is required to answer to the enemy's Artillery firing, shelling on our Infantry, in first or second line, it is often omitted to let our Artillery know the results that seem to be given on the enemy's batteries.

"How, when a counter-firing has been required for, it may happen that the shelling made by the enemy:—

>Goes on without change.
>Goes on more weakly.
>Or stops completely.

"In those three cases it is necessary to warn the Artillery:—

"In the first case it is certain that the enemy's battery that is shelling is not struck, the firing must, of course, be modified.

"In the second one, it may be admitted that the enemy's firing is troubled, but the counter-firing must go further on.

"In the third one, the enemy's firing being stopped, it is necessary to stop our firing, in order to avoid the useless expense of ammunition.

"This note is to be given in communication to all Infantry Officers."

General Commander of the 18th Division,
(Signed) LEFEVRE.

F.A.,
The Chief of the Staff.

1st LIFE GUARDS

Owing to the proximity of their own trenches (the opposing lines varied from 100 yards to 40 yards apart), the enemy were unable to shell the position.

A remarkable feature of the position, due to the fact that the trenches were originally part of the German line, was an old communication trench running from the centre of the line (held by B Squadron) straight into the German lines.

At night small parties of the enemy were able to creep up this to within a few yards of our position, and cut wire. It was only when Verey pistols and flares were issued on February 6th that this trouble could be satisfactorily dealt with.

Part of the section occupied by D Squadron on the left was subject to enfilade fire. This was difficult to guard against, as owing to the wet state of this trench the parapets were constantly sinking. It was here that most of the casualties occurred.

Feb. 8th.

The Regiment remained in the advanced trenches till the evening of February 8, when the relief was carried out in accordance with B.M. 86.

The Regiment when relieved, took over the billets of 1st Royal Dragoons in RUE DES CHIENS YPRES.

B.M. 86.

To 1st Life Guards.

"Reliefs to-night as follows:—

"1st Life Guards by Royals commencing midnight, Leicesters by Somersets 12.30 a.m., 2nd Life Guards by 3rd Dragoon Guards 1.0 a.m., Royal Horse Guards and Essex by 10th Hussars and Essex 1.30 a.m. Filled belts for machine-guns, and boxes for same will be handed over to relieving Regiments. No 7th Cavalry Brigade transport is coming but General Supply waggons of 6th Cavalry Brigade will wait in ZILLEBEKE, and one waggon will be at disposal of each Regiment and will march with it to billets. When relieved each Regiment will march independently to billets, being met by billeting party opposite Divisional Headquarters."

From 7th Cavalry Brigade.

1st LIFE GUARDS.
CASUALTY LIST.

922	Private Brooks, H.,	3rd Dragoon Guards,	*Killed*	4/2/15
5832	„ Cotton, F.,	6th Dragoons,	*Wounded*	5/2/15
2670	Trooper Rhodes, W.,	1st Life Guards,	„	5/2/15
8332	Private Marshall, W.,	3rd Dragoon Guards,	„	6/2/15
	Surgeon-Major R. M. Cowie,	1st Life Guards,	„	7/2/15
5614	Corporal Brunsden, J.,	6th Dragoons,	*Killed*	8/2/15

Ypres—Feb. 11.—Nothing of interest or importance occurred while the Regiment was in YPRES, between February 8th-11th. About 8.30 p.m. on 11th, however, the enemy started shelling the town in the immediate vicinity of RUE DES CHIENS. In all 10 shells were fired, of which 3 failed to explode. One fell in a house occupied by a troop of D Squadron. Half the house was wrecked, and the following casualties were the result:—

5644	Corporal Cordery, H.,	6th Dragoons	*Killed*	11/2/15
2501	Private Williams, R. J.,	„	„	„
5400	„ Corcoran, J.,	„	„	„
6446	„ Hall, J.,	2nd Dragoon Guards,	„	„

WAR DIARY OF

5128	Private	Sullivan, M.,	2nd Dragoons,	*Killed*	11/2/15
5972	,,	Smith,	1st King's Dragoon Guards,	,,	,,
2513	,,	Higgins, E.,	6th Dragoons,	*Wounded*	,,
6314	,,	Leslie, R.,	1st King's Dragoon Guards,	,,	,,
5466	,,	Crane, C.,	6th Dragoons,	,,	,,
4753	,,	Pitt, T.,	3rd Dragoon Guards,	,,	,,
5208	,,	Finch, M.,	6th Dragoons,	,,	,,
6227	,,	Pigrum, E.,	1st King's Dragoon Guards,	,,	,,
6642	,,	Gilchrist, A.,	6th Dragoons,	,,	,,
6427	,,	Cummings, J.,	2nd Dragoon Guards,	,,	,,

Feb. 12.—The Regiment returned with the rest of Brigade to original billets at EBBLINGHEM on being relieved by 2nd Cavalry Division the Regiment's billets in RUE DES CHIENS being taken over by the Carabiniers (4th Cavalry Brigade).

B.M. 100.

To 1st Life Guards.

"7th Cavalry Brigade and detachment 8th Cavalry Brigade will return to HAZEBROUCK area to-morrow evening, 12th inst., by motor-buses which bring up relieving Regiments. Units of 8th Cavalry Brigade will form up in mass at E. end of GRANDE PLACE (the square), YPRES, at 6 p.m. Units of 7th Cavalry Brigade each in column of route in the streets in which they are billeted, heads at corners leading into the square. As much kit and equipment as possible to be taken with men in buses, but a lorry will be at the disposal of each Brigade if required. 8th Cavalry Brigade will enter buses first. 7th Cavalry Brigade Order—1st Life Guards, 2nd Life Guards, Leicester Yeomanry, Brigade Headquarters.

From 7th Cavalry Brigade.   D. P. TOLLEMACHE, Captain.

Nothing of note occurred during the following week, during which the Regiment remained at EBBLINGHEM.

Ebblinghem—Feb. 19.—The under-mentioned Officers, N.C.O.'s and men appeared in the list of those mentioned in despatches in connection with the despatch from the Field-Marshal Commanding-in-Chief, dated November 20th, 1914, and dealing with the battle of YPRES—ARMENTIERES, published in *The London Gazette*, February 17th, 1915 :—

STANLEY, Major Hon. A. F., D.S.O.
GROSVENOR, Capt. Lord H. W.
HARDY, Capt. L. H. (Military Cross).
WYNDHAM, Capt. Hon. E. H.
ROANTREE, No. 5454 Sergeant J.
LIDSTER, No. 5375 Corpl. F., 6th Dragoons.
SWAIN, No. 4870 Trooper G., 5th Dragoon Guards.
WHITTAKER, No. 2741 Trooper S.

The under-mentioned Officers of the Regiment were mentioned for services performed with the Composite Regiment of Household Cavalry :—

WYNDHAM, Capt. Hon. E. S., D.S.O.
SMITH, Lieut. A. L. E. (Military Cross).

In publishing the above list in Regimental Orders, the Commanding Officer took the opportunity of drawing attention to the names of the under-mentioned N.C.O. and men, who at different times had been brought to the notice of the Brigadier for gallant and distinguished conduct :—

2570 Corpl. A. FABRAY.
2617 Trooper H. HAYDEN.
2442 Trooper S. CLEMENTS.
6339 Private A. HIBBERD.

Feb. 23.—The Regiment furnished a party of 3 Officers, 100 men, and 3 servants to assist in looking after the horses of 1st Cavalry

1st LIFE GUARDS

Division during the time the latter were in the trenches near ZILLEBEKE. This party proceeded by motor-bus to BERTHEN, under the command of Major Sir F. CARDEN, Bart.

Feb. 24.—The Regiment furnished a party of 100 rank and file to assist in digging a line of defence near LA BELLE HOTESSE, this being the line on which the allied armies would fall back in the event of the present line having to be evacuated.

Feb. 25.—A similar party to the above was again furnished under same arrangements.

Feb. 26.—Owing to a horse inspection by the D.D.V.S. Cavalry Corps, no working party was furnished this day.

Feb. 27 and 28.—Working parties were again furnished as before, strength 70 men on 27th and 125 on 28th. The following War Office letter bears on a matter which has hitherto greatly exercised the minds of the troops during the campaign.

EXTRACT FROM WAR OFFICE LETTER W.O. (S) 18/2/15.

"PLUM AND APPLE JAM.

"We are now sending other kinds of jam and some marmalade and at the end of the week the marmalade will probably be coming in in very large quantities. I would suggest that Base Depots be told to issue anything in the way of jam they have except plum and apple and to hold that back even if by doing so they may be issuing their newest stocks, as after all jam will keep for a considerable period. At the end of a month or two when the troops are tired of marmalade they will probably greet the plum and apple as an old and welcome friend."

March 1—9.—Nothing of note occurred. On March 6th the party under Major Sir F. CARDEN, which had been looking after horses of 1st Cavalry Division returned on completion of that duty.

B.M. 3.

To 1st Life Guards.

"Regiments fighting troops including A Echelon will be prepared to move from Regimental rendezvous at one hour's notice after receipt of order commencing from 6 a.m. to-morrow. Brigade rendezvous, LA KREULE. Order of march: Leicester Yeomanry, 2nd Life Guards, 1st Life Guards. 1st Life Guards and 2nd Life Guards will march with their A Echelon and drop this behind A Echelon of Leicester Yeomanry, the head of which will be at LA BREARDE until the Brigade moves off from LA KREULE. Tools will be distributed to Regimental Headquarters by a Divisional Lorry about 6 a.m. Squadrons will saddle up at 6 a.m., then A Echelon will be packed. Unless move previously ordered B Echelon will be packed at 8 a.m."

From 7th Cavalry Brigade. D. P. TOLLEMACHE, Captain.

March 10.—Regiment stood to all day in accordance with B.M. 3.

This was due to the fact that the First Army were attacking the enemy.

SPECIAL ORDER.

To the First Army.

"We are about to engage the enemy under very favourable conditions. Until now in the present campaign, the British Army has, by its pluck and determination, gained victories against an enemy greatly superior both in men and guns. Reinforcements have made us stronger than the enemy in our front. Our guns are now both more numerous than the enemy's are, and also larger than any hitherto used by any army in the field. Our Flying Corps has driven the Germans from the air.

"On the Eastern Front, and to the South of us, our Allies have made marked progress and caused enormous losses to the Germans, who are, moreover, harassed by internal troubles and shortage of supplies, so that there is little prospect at present of big reinforcements being sent against us here.

"In front of us we have only one German Corps, spread out on a front as large as that occupied by the whole of our Army (the First).

"We are now about to attack with about 48 battalions a locality in that front which is held by some three German battalions. It seems probable, also, that for the first day of the operations the Germans will not have more than four battalions available as reinforcements for the counter attack. Quickness of movement is therefore of first importance to enable us to forestall the enemy and thereby gain success without severe loss.

"At no time in this war has there been a more favourable moment for us, and I feel confident of success. The extent of that success must depend on the rapidity and determination with which we advance.

"Although fighting in France, let us remember that we are fighting to preserve the British Empire and to protect our homes against the organised savagery of the German Army. To ensure success, each one of us must play his part, and fight like men for the Honour of Old England."

9th March, 1915.   (Signed) D. HAIG, General, Commanding 1st Army.

March 11.

B.M. 9.

To 1st Life Guards.

"The Brigade will form with head at LA KREULE at 6.15 a.m. to-morrow.

"B Echelon will move forward to LA BREARDE by 7 a.m. where Brigade Transport Officer will take charge.

"NEUVE CHAPELLE officially reported taken. 250 prisoners.

"6 p.m. We had advanced about 500 yards at NEUVE CHAPELLE."

Regiment moved in accordance with B.M. 9 to a point $\frac{1}{4}$ of a mile N.E. of LA MOTTE station as mobile reserve. Whole of 3rd Cavalry Division in these woods.

La Motte—March 11, 4 p.m.—Regiment ordered to billet round ARREWAGE.

A 2.

To Squadrons.

"Regiment will be saddled up at 5.30 a.m. ready to move at short notice. In event of a move Regiment will assemble with head at road junction at *T* in ARRET in order D, A, MG, B. Echelon A in rear. Brigade order of march—2nd Life Guards, 1st Life Guards, Leicesters, Echelon A. Send all limbered wagons to road junction ¾ mile S.E. of *T* in ARRET at once to draw rations."

Arrewage—March 12, 5.30 A.M.

Regiment saddled up ready to move in accordance with A 2. Did not move during the day.

From 1st Life Guards, Arrewage, 6.10 p.m.

E. H. WYNDHAM, Captain, Adjutant 1st Life Guards.

B.M. 10.

To 1st Life Guards.

"Regiments will be saddled up in billets from 6 a.m. to-morrow, ready for immediate concentration for move in S.E. direction. Officers' spare horses and watercarts to accompany A Echelon. If regiments move B Echelon will pack and await orders.

"News to-day—20th Brigade have crossed road leading N.W. from MOULIN DE PIETRE and are pushing on towards RUE D'ENFER. They report capture of several hundred prisoners and state that Germans are still surrendering. It is believed that 1,100 prisoners have been taken to-day, and 5 field guns."

From 7th Cavalry Brigade.   D. P. TOLLEMACHE, Captain.

March 13, 6 A.M.—Regiment saddled up in accordance with B.M. 10.

1st LIFE GUARDS

B.M. 11 and B.M. 12 received during morning.

B.M. 11.

To 1st Life Guards.

"If Regiments march B Echelon, in default of further orders, will be concentrated in Regimental billeting areas and each regiment will send a cyclist orderly to Brigade Headquarters to report to the Brigade Transport Officer (Captain Meade) to remain with him for purpose of conveying orders to their Regimental Transport (B Echelon)."

From 7th Cavalry Brigade.

D. P. TOLLEMACHE, Captain.

B.M. 12.

To 1st Life Guards.

"The Brigade will be ready to move off from Brigade rendezvous at 2 hours' notice from receipt of orders at Brigade Headquarters. Regiments may therefore off saddle, but must be prepared to reach Brigade rendezvous within 1½ hour of orders reaching Regimental Headquarters."

From 7th Cavalry Brigade, 9.40 a.m.

D. P. TOLLEMACHE, Captain.

Reinforcements received:—Lieutenant Sir R. V. SUTTON, 2nd Lieutenant C. E. TRAFFORD, and 3 other ranks.

March 13, 6.30 P.M.

Regiment moved in accordance with B.M. 14, the billets at ARREWAGE being taken over by 12th Lancers.

Owing to roads being very much blocked with transport, it was found impossible to form up the Brigade, and Regiments accordingly marched independently to old billets.

B.M. 14.

To 1st Life Guards.

"Brigade will return to old billets to-night, move to commence 6.30 p.m. At 5 p.m. B Echelon will be formed with head at road junction LA RUE DU BOIS. The Brigade with A Echelon will be formed at the same hour with head at Cross-roads ½ mile S.W. of S in SWARTENBROUCK. Order of march—Leicester Yeomanry, 1st Life Guards, 2nd Life Guards. B Echelon will move to starting-point by road running through 3rd E of VERTE RUE, leaving the road through the 1st E clear for fighting troops. Supplies will be dumped at old billets."

From 7th Cavalry Brigade.

D. P. TOLLEMACHE, Captain.

Ebblinghem—March 14.—B.M. 15.

B.M. 15.

To 1st Life Guards.

"The Regiments of this Brigade will stand prepared to concentrate at Cross-roads immediately S. of HONDEGHEM in 2 hours from receipt of order at Regimental Headquarters.

"1st Life Guards behind 2nd Life Guards on HONDEGHEM—STAPLE road."

From 7th Cavalry Brigade.

D. P. TOLLEMACHE, Captain.

March 15.

Regiment concentrated in accordance with B.M. 18, at 10.30 a.m.

Brigade, however, was not called upon to move, and Regiment returned to billets in course of afternoon. Above precautionary measures were due to somewhat heavy fighting on the front of 27th Division at ST. ELOI.

WAR DIARY OF

B.M. 18.

To 1st Life Guards.

"The Brigade has orders to be ready so that head of Brigade shall move off from Brigade rendezvous within 40 minutes of receipt of order at Brigade Headquarters. Therefore Regiments will concentrate immediately on receipt of the present message. Leicester Yeomanry head at Cross-roads immediately S. of HONDEGHEM, 1st Life Guards head at LONGUE CROIX, 2nd Life Guards head at STAPLE. Order of march—Leicester Yeomanry, 1st Life Guards, 2nd Life Guards. B Echelon will assemble in Regimental rendezvous ready to move at one hour's notice if the Brigade is ordered to march. If Brigade marches each Regiment will send cyclist orderly to report to Brigade Transport Officer at Brigade Headquarters."

From 7th Cavalry Brigade.

D. P. TOLLEMACHE, Captain.

March 16.—Squadrons saddled up and concentrated at Squadron Headquarters at 6.30 a.m., Brigade having been warned to concentrate within 1 hour and 40 minutes from receipt of order at Brigade Headquarters. About 10.30 a.m. Squadrons were allowed to off saddle and return to troop billets.

March 17.—Brigade ordered to concentrate within 3 hours and 50 minutes of receipt of order. It was therefore unnecessary for Squadrons to saddle up.

March 18-31.—Regiment remained in billets. Nothing to report.

The following reinforcements were received during the month of March:—

March 2.—6 other ranks.

March 11.—2nd Lieutenant G. T. TRAFFORD and 3 other ranks.

March 12.—Captain Sir R. V. SUTTON.

March 13.—Lieutenant G. DRUMMOND.
2nd Lieutenant R. G. THYNNE.
2nd Lieutenant COUNT J. DE SALIS.
5 other ranks.

March 22.—6 other ranks.

The following Officers were evacuated:—

March 15.—Captain ST. G. CLOWES.
Lieutenant H. H. ALDRIDGE.
2nd Lieutenant T. NOTTIDGE.

March 26.—2nd Lieutenant R. G. THYNNE.
2nd Lieutenant COUNT J. DE SALIS.

Ebblinghem—April 1-11.—Nothing to report.

Ebblinghem—April 12.—Regiment moved from previous billets to area between WALLONCAPPEL and RENESCURE south of Railway. Regimental Headquarters moved to Chateau, 1 kilometre E. of EBBLINGHEM Station.

1st LIFE GUARDS

Ebblinghem—April 19.—Major-General C. T. McM. KAVANAGH, on leaving the Brigade to take up command of 2nd Cavalry Division, published the following order :—

"On leaving the 7th Cavalry Brigade Major General KAVANAGH wishes to thank all ranks for the loyal support they have invariably given him since he took over command, and while bidding them good-bye he wishes them the best of luck and success in the future."

Ebblinghem—April 23, 1.15 P.M.—Brigade marched from LES CINQ RUES via LE BREARDE—CAESTRE—GODEWAERSVELDE to a position of readiness at ABEELE. This move was occasioned by the attack by the enemy with the aid of asphyxiating gases on the French position about LANGEMARCK.

At 9 p.m. billeted at GODEWAERSVELDE.

Godewaersvelde—April 24, 8 A.M.—Brigade marched via BOESCHEPE and RENINGHELST to Point 35, where it remained in reserve all day.

At nightfall retired to billets about INN on POPERINGHE—WESTOUTRE road.

B.M.3.
To 1st Life Guards.

The Brigade will rendezvous at 8.30 a.m. to-morrow at crossroads ½ mile N. of H in RENINGHELST, and will mass clear of the road.

Regiments will be prepared to move off from same rendezvous 1½ hour after receipt of order at any time between now and 8 a.m.

Supplies at WESTOUTRE for 2nd Life Guards, at RENINGHELST for Leicester Yeomanry, at INN for 1st Life Guards.

Inn—April 25, 8.30 A.M.—Brigade moved to position of readiness in accordance with B.M.3.

About 1 p.m. moved through POPERINGHE to HAMHOEK.

At 6 p.m. withdrew to billets between WATOU and WINNEZEELE.

Watou—April 26, 6 A.M.—Brigade moved to position of readiness on the Frontier on WINNEZEELE road.

At noon moved to FORGE 2 miles S.E. of WATOU.

At 7 p.m. marched to a farm 1 mile W. of POPERINGHE on FORGE—POPERINGHE road where the horses were left and 13 officers and 273 other ranks marched to wooden huts at VLAMERTINGHE.

SPECIAL ORDER OF THE DAY.

The Field Marshal Commanding-in-Chief has received the following message from the Secretary, War Office :—

To Sir John French,
General Headquarters.   *April 24th,* 1915.

His Majesty sends the following message :

"During the past week I have followed with admiration the splendid achievements of my troops including the capture and retention of Hill 60 after heavy fighting, and the gallant conduct of the Canadian Division in repulsing the enemy and recapturing four heavy guns. I heartily congratulate all units who have taken part in these successful actions."

Vlamertinghe—April 27.—Remained in the huts. During the afternoon VLAMERTINGHE was shelled, and the following casualties occurred :—

Killed.—2947 Corpl. W. CLAY, 2427 Corpl. of Horse G. MCFEELEY, 2905 Tr. R. W. WESTLEY. *Wounded.*—6095 Tr. E. MCCULLEN.

WAR DIARY OF

In view of this, Brigade moved from the huts to the fields ½-mile further south, where they spent the night.

Vlamertinghe—April 28, 2 P.M.—Brigade marched back to point where horses had been left and billeted at Cross Roads 1 mile N.W. of ABEELE.

Forge—April 29, 8.30 A.M.—Brigade concentrated at FORGE in accordance with B.M.11.

> B.M.11.
>
> *To* 1st Life Guards.
>
> Regiments will march so as to reach Brigade rendezvous (FORGE), at 8.30 a.m., and on arriving there will form on either side of road S. of FORGE, as before, with 1st and 2nd Life Guards, E. of road and Leicester Yeomanry and A echelon W. of it. Order of march—2nd Life Guards, 1st Life Guards, Leicester Yeomanry. Field Ambulance to reach "T" road south of FORGE at 9 a.m. and remain with head at that point.
>
> *From* 7th Cavalry Brigade.   D. P. T.

Remained there all day and returned to same billets in evening.

> B.M.12.
>
> *To* 1st Life Guards.
>
> Regiments will return to same billets. Be prepared to reach Brigade rendezvous—road junction ½-mile N. of 1st H. in HILLEHOEK, 1¾ hrs. after orders reach Brigade Headquarters.
>
> Order of March—1st Life Guards, Leicester Yeomanry, 2nd Life Guards.
>
> Supplies at same place as last night, except that 2nd Life Guards supplies will, *if possible*, be brought to Signal Office opposite Brigade Headquarters.
>
> If no previous move ordered, Brigade will rendezvous at 8.30 a.m. at above-mentioned road junction, and will then form up in fields as to-day, and off saddle.
>
> *From* 7th Cavalry Brigade.

Forge—April 30.—Programme of April 29th repeated.

Forge—May 1.—Programme of two previous days repeated.

Forge—May 2.—After spending the day at FORGE billeted at ST. JAN-TER-BIEZEN.

St. Jan-ter-Biezen—May 3, 4.30 P.M.—Brigade marched in accordance with B.M.19.

> B.M.19.
>
> *To* 1st Life Guards.
>
> The Brigade will rendezvous at 4.30 p.m. with head at crossroads 1 mile E. of WATOU and N. of R. of WARANDEBECK stream. Order of march—1st Life Guards, Leicester Yeomanry, 2nd Life Guards.
>
> Billeting parties will meet regiments as under—1st Life Guards at road junction ½ mile W. of the H. of HERZEELE—Leicester Yeomanry at road junction ¼ mile N.E. of L. of BRIEL, 2nd Life Guards at crossroads ¾ mile N.W. of H. of HOOTKERQUE.
>
> Brigade Headquarters will be at HERZEELE.

Just as the march started it was recalled and marched to VLAMERTINGHE, which was reached at nightfall. Here the horses were left, and 13 officers and about 260 other ranks marched to a point midway between VLAMERTINGHE and YPRES.

Vlamertinghe—May 4, 6 A.M.—After waiting here till 6 a.m. returned to the horses, and marched to area mentioned in B.M.19 above.

Road Junction ½-mile W. of H in Herzeele—May 5.—Remained in billets all day. Working party under command of Capt. E. HELY found in accordance with B.M.21.

1st LIFE GUARDS

B.M.21.

To 1st Life Guards.

The working parties to-day will be formed as follows : 1st Life Guards, 2nd Life Guards, and Leicester Yeomanry ; each 3 officers, a proportion of N.C.Os. and 67 men to dig. These parties will go up mounted, under a Field Officer to be detailed by O.C. 1st Life Guards.

One mounted horse holder to each N.C.O. or man of the working parties, to accompany the parties to the point where horses will be left. No tools will be carried with mounted parties. Men to take rifle, one bandolier, mackintosh instead of cloak, emergency rations, feeds for horses.

Working parties to rendezvous at crossroads on HERZEELE-HOUTKERQUE road, midway between those two places, at 3.20 p.m.

Parties will return in early morning—remainder of Brigade will remain in billets.

From 7th Cavalry Brigade. 1.40 p.m.

D. P. T.

Brigadier-General A. A. KENNEDY took over command of the Brigade.

Herzeele—May 6.—Remained in billets all day. Working party returned from YPRES in early morning.

Herzeele—May 7, 4.50 P.M.— Marched back to approximately old billeting area near EBBLINGHEM.

B.M.22.

1st Life Guards.

2nd Life Guards.

Leicestershire Yeomanry.

May 7th.—The Brigade will march to billets in the area HAZEBROUCK (exclusive), EBBLINGHEM (ex.), LYNDE (inclus.), B des HUIT RUES—Le Gd. HASARD in following order, via STEENVOORDE.

UNIT.	STARTING POINT.	TIME.
B.H.Q.	Crossroads by E. of LE NOUVEAU MONDE.	4.45 p.m.
Leicestershire Yeomanry	Do.	4.45 ,,
1st Life Guards	Do.	4.50 ,,
2nd Life Guards	Do.	4.55 ,,
A Echelon transport in order of march of units	Do.	5.0 ,,
7th Cavalry Field Ambulance	Do.	5.5 ,,

The Eastern portion of the area is allotted to the Leicestershire Yeomanry.

The Centre ,, ,, 2nd Life Guards.

The Western ,, ,, 1st Life Guards.

B.H.Q. will be established at the CHATEAU midway between WALLONCAPPEL and SERCUS.

Regiments are to report to B.H.Q. as above as soon as all their troops are in billets.

While in billets troops are to remain ready to turn out at one hour's notice.

If ordered to concentrate, Regiments will do so at the crossroads on the main HAZEBROUCK-AIRE road by the E. of LA CUNEWELE, moving into fields by the roadside on arrival.

D. P. TOLLEMACHE, Captain Brigade Major.

To 1st Life Guards.

Following received from Cavalry Corps 9 a.m. begins : "In the vicinity of Hill 60 we recaptured during the night one of the lost trenches on the Salient and were endeavouring to capture the remainder at time of last report. At 3 a.m. the enemy collected in part of trenches on MENIN Road but were dispersed by our Artillery fire which was very effective." (Ends.)

From 7th Cavalry Brigade.

To 1st Life Guards.

Copy of message from 3rd Cavalry Division. First Cavalry Division comes under orders of 2nd Army from 6 a.m. to-day. 2nd and 3rd Cavalry Divisions will return this afternoon to approximately the original billeting areas near HAZEBROUCK. No movement to take place till further orders. Designation Plumer's Force will be discontinued. General Allenby has been appointed to command 5th Corps. General Byng to Cavalry Corps. General Briggs to 3rd Cavalry Division.

From 3rd Cavalry Division, 7.0 a.m. 7th Cavalry Brigade.

WAR DIARY OF

Ebblinghem—May 8.—One hour's notice to turn out increased to three hours.

Ebblinghem—May 9, 12 NOON.—Regiment moved in accordance with B.M.26. 9.30 a.m.

> *To* 1st Life Guards, Leicestershire Yeomanry, 2nd Life Guards.
> B.M.26.
>
> *May 9.* — The Brigade will proceed by motor-buses to the vicinity of VLAMERTINGE Units embarking at the points mentioned as quickly as possible.
>
> 1st Life Guards embark on road just E. of EBBLINGHEM Station.
>
> 2nd Life Guards embark Crossroads N. of WALLON CAPPEL.
>
> Leicestershire Yeomanry embark LES CINQ RUES.
>
> One-third of officers to be left with horses and men in proportion of one to four horses. Machine guns and belt boxes—two bandoliers—cloak or mackintosh, iron ration to be taken. A Echelon and pack transport will follow the buses under orders of Major BARRY.
>
> B Echelon remains in billets.
>
> All buses are now at EBBLINGHEM and are being brought under brigade arrangement to the points mentioned for embarking.
>
> A Echelon vehicles will probably be left just west of POPERINGHE and pack horses will probably be brought up to VLAMERTINGHE.
>
> There are twelve buses for each Regiment.
>
> D. P. TOLLEMACHE,, Brigade Major,
> 7th Cavalry Brigade.

On arrival at VLAMERTINGHE it occupied huts between the former and BRIELEN. Digging party was found in accordance with B.M.29 to dig on line of defence running along YPRES Canal.

> B.M.29.
> 1st Life Guards.
> 2nd Life Guards.
> Leicestershire Yeomanry.
>
> The Brigade has to find 600 men for digging to-night. Each Regiment will find a working party of 200 men, with a proportion of officers and N.C.O's. These parties will fall in East of the huts at 8 p.m. and a Brigade Staff Officer will lead them to the rendezvous (BEGERSBURG CHATEAU in H. 6b).
>
> Remainder of men will stay in huts and will unload supplies from limbers when these arrive.
>
> The tools for digging are coming up in limbered waggons under Divisional arrangements.
>
> D. P. TOLLEMACHE, Captain,
> Brigade-Major.

Vlamertinghe—May 10.—Remained all day in huts.

Vlamertinghe—May 11. — Following officers proceeded to take over trenches in accordance with B.M.37 :—Lieutenant H. HULTON-HARROP, Lieutenant G. H. DRUMMOND, 2nd Lieutenant J. S. WOOLLEY. Six other ranks joined B Echelon from base.

> *To* 1st Life Guards.
> 1st and 2nd Life Guards. Leicestershire Yeomanry.
> B.M.37.
>
> *May 11th.*—The 3rd Cavalry Division is to relieve the 80th Brigade in the trenches East of YPRES to-morrow night.
>
> Each regiment will detail one officer per squadron to proceed to-night to the level crossing (square I.11.b) where they will be met by officers of the 80th Brigade and shewn the trenches which they are to take over.
>
> The officers detailed should be at these Headquarters ready to start at 7.30 p.m. when further instructions will be given them.
>
> D. P. TOLLEMACHE, Captain,
> Brigade-Major 7th Cavalry Brigade.

1st LIFE GUARDS

4.53 p.m.

To 1st and 2nd Life Guards, Leicestershire Yeomanry.

B.M. *May 12th.*

The Brigade will proceed dismounted at 7.30 p.m. via YPRES to POTIJZE. Order of march Leicestershire Yeomanry, 2nd Life Guards, 1st Life Guards.

Each Regiment will be followed by its own pack transport.

On arrival at POTIJZE, Guides from the 85th Brigade will conduct Regiment to their trenches.

The front allotted to the Brigade extends from the YPRES—ROULERS railway exclusive (sq. I. 6c) to the YPRES—VERLORENHOEK road—exclusive. The 6th Cavalry Brigade is on the right and the 1st Cavalry Division on the left of this portion of the line.

The front will be divided equally between the three Regiments of the Brigade—Leicestershire Yeomanry on right, 2nd Life Guards in centre and 1st Life Guards on left. Each Regiment having 2 squadrons in front line and 1 in support—about 100 yards in rear.

A Echelon transport with ammunition, tools and R.E. stores is being taken under Divisional arrangements to the vicinity of the dug-outs by the railway crossing (I. 11B). Regiments should send representatives to this locality after reaching the trenches to carry up the ammunition, tools and R.E. stores. Water carts accompany A Echelon.

B.H.Q. will be at POTIJZE Chateau, where also are those of the 8th Cavalry Brigade in reserve.

Brigade-Major, 7th Cavalry Brigade.

6.30 p.m.

A.K.83.

To 1st Life Guards.

Commander 5th corps wishes it to be clearly understood that line now held by 1st and 3rd Cavalry divisions must be maintained and that in case of enemy affecting a lodgment anywhere in the line a counter attack must at once be made to keep the line intact.

Kindly say whether you wish your reinforcements left in huts brought up to-morrow night. All supplies have now been dumped here instead of at level crossing dug-outs.

You must send here to fetch what you require and arrange to keep one man each here as guide.

From 7th Cavalry Brigade, Potijze, 12.30.

1st LIFE GUARDS.

Reinforcements :—

*2838	Trooper Stribling, B.	1st Life Guards	..	11/5/15.
*6255	Private Legg, W. ..	1st Dragoon Guards		,,
*6241	,, Hockley, A. ..	,,		,,
*4025	,, Milner, R. ..	3rd Dragoon Guards		,,
*2495	,, Daly, J. ..	6th Dragoons	..	,,
*5592	,, Berryman F.	13th Hussars	..	,,
	Capt. J. C. G. Leigh ..	1st Life Guards	..	14/5/15.
6974	Sh. Sm. Alderton, G. F.	13th Hussars	..	,,
*2458	C. of H. Wright, A.	1st Life Guards	..	15/5/15.
*5382	Private Torrens, J. ..	6th Dragoons	..	,,
*2403	Trooper Grace, W. ..	1st Life Guards	..	,,
*5517	Private Collier A.	1st Dragoons ..	..	,,
*8416	,, Packer, W. ..	6th Dragoon Guards		,,
*3041	Trooper Sanders, J.	1st Life Guards	..	16/5/15.
*2647	Corporal Utton C. ..	,,	..	17/5/15.
*2552	Trooper McFeeley E.	,,	..	18/5/15.

* From Hospital.

Vlamertinghe—May 12.—Regiment took over trenches in accordance with Brigade Orders and A.K.83. The line taken over was not that mentioned in B.M.37 above, but further north at VERLOREN HOEK. Regiment relieved a battalion of EAST SURREY Regiment. On taking over news was received that Lieutenant H. HULTON-HARROP had been killed in the trenches during the day. Just as the relief was completed 2nd Lieutenant J. S. WOOLLEY was wounded. Following officers were in trenches night of 12th-13th: Lieut.-Col. Hon. A. F. STANLEY, D.S.O., Captain G. E. M. MUNDY, Captain J. J. ASTOR, Captain R. HAMILTON-STUBBER, Captain and Adjutant Hon. E. H. WYNDHAM, Captain Sir R. V. SUTTON, Lieutenant G. H.

Drummond, 2nd Lieutenant M. Seton-Karr, 2nd Lieutenant J. S. Woolley, 2nd Lieutenant T. K. Robson, 2nd Lieutenant S. C. Bostock, Surg.-Lieut. E. D. Anderson.

The left of the position occupied by the regiment rested on the Ypres—Zonnebeke road and was some 150 yards in advance of the front trenches occupied by the Queen's Bays on the north of the road. This was a source of weakness, as the line could be enfiladed from some houses just north of the road, which it was not easy to deny to the enemy should they advance.

This section of the line was occupied by B Squadron with D Squadron and Headquarters in a support trench 50 yards in rear. When regiment took over, these two trenches were not joined by a communicating trench. This however was dug during the night.

On the right of B Squadron was a gap in the line of some 150 yards in which a farm was situated. South of the farm was A Squadron joining on the right with 2nd Life Guards.

One Machine Gun under 2nd Lieutenant Bostock was posted in B Squadron trench, the other with twenty men of A Squadron under 2nd Lieutenant M. Seton-Karr was posted in a farm 300 yards in rear of the position to form a *point d'appui*.

Potijze—May 13, 3.30 a.m.—The enemy's guns began to register on the position. At 4 a.m. a very heavy bombardment commenced, and lasted with unabated vigour till 7 a.m. This was unquestionably the heaviest bombardment the regiment had ever experienced during the campaign. The enemy's "*Minenwerfer*" were particularly effective. At 7 a.m. the enemy's infantry advanced. They did not appear to be in any great strength, and made no frontal attacks on the front of B Squadron, but made for the houses on the left beforementioned.

About 7.10 a.m. it was noticed that the right of the Brigade line was retiring, A Squadron was involved in this retirement. Regiment less A Squadron hung on for another ten minutes, when it was forced to retire, both flanks being threatened.

They rallied behind a mound 100 yards in rear of the support trench, but the enemy advanced feebly and presented no target. From this position regiment moved to the left into the front trenches of the Queen's Bays, where they remained all day.

Meanwhile A Squadron retired on General Headquarters line, which was occupied by the Divisional Reserve. No. 2048 Corporal of Horse G. Attenborough and four men remained in a large shell hole just in front of the *point d'appui* (which had been destroyed by enemy's guns) until 10th Hussars counter-attacked at 2.30 p.m. when they joined in the counter-attack.

1st LIFE GUARDS

Throughout the day Headquarters B and D Squadrons remained in Bays' trenches, and all ranks owe a deep debt of gratitude to the latter regiment for the magnificent support and assistance they gave to the regiment throughout a very trying day.

Throughout the day the trenches were very heavily shelled. In all the enemy's guns fired on the position for sixteen consecutive hours. Position lost in morning retaken by brilliant counter-attack by 8th Cavalry Brigade at 2.30 p.m. but they were unable to hold it, retiring again about 4 p.m.

G.69.
To Officer Commanding 1st Life Guards.

You should bring your regiment to Divisional Headquarters and report to G.O.C. 7th Brigade in his dug-out which adjoins.

8.45 p.m.
M. F. GAGE, Lieut.-Col.

At 8.30 p.m. regiment retired to POTIJZE in accordance with G.69.

1st LIFE GUARDS.
CASUALTY RETURN, 12TH AND 13TH MAY, 1915.

Lieutenant H. Hulton Harrop			Killed	12/5/15.
Lieutenant J. S. Woolley			Wounded	,,
3054 Trooper Abrahams, M.		1st Life Guards	Killed	13/5/15.
2807 Corporal Kimpton, E.		,,	,,	,,
2929 Trooper Roberts, W. H.		,,	,,	,,
2818 ,, Pearce, C.		,,	,,	,,
2891 Corporal Rowe, C.		,,	,,	,,
2817 Trooper Golding, G.		,,	,,	,,
2802 Corporal Castle, E.		,,	,,	,,
2666 Trooper Flaxman, W.		,,	,,	,,
2859 ,, Russell, C.		,,	,,	,,
2714 ,, Arnold, A.		,,	,,	,,
3103 ,, Moores, J.		,,	,,	,,
3080 ,, Pye, O.		,,	,,	,,
2916 Corporal Gibson A.		,,	,,	,,
2287 Trooper Ruscoe, A.		,,	,,	,,
2326 C. of H. Coates, J.		,,	,,	,,
2741 Trooper Whittaker, S.		,,	,,	,,
5466 Corporal Crane, C.		6th Dragoons	,,	,,
5612 Private Meredith		,,	,,	,,
4934 ,, Harvey, W.		2nd D. Guards	,,	,,
5787 ,, Harvey, G.		,,	,,	,,
5066 ,, Ramage, E.		5th D. Guards	,,	,,
4786 ,, Duffy, R.		,,	,,	,,
5548 ,, Heyes, F.		6th Dragoons	,,	,,
5044 ,, Slater, E.		3rd D. Guards	,,	,,
Capt. Sir R. V. Sutton, Bt.		1st Life Guards	Wounded	,,
Lieut. G. H. Drummond		,,	,,	,,
2nd Lieut. M. Seton-Kerr		,,	,,	,,
2nd Lieut. S. C. Bostock		,,	,,	,,
3038 C. of H. Storey, G.		,,	,,	,,
2548 ,, Wilcox, P.		,,	,,	,,
2803 Corporal Bowler E.		,,	,,	,,
2899 ,, Marriage, W.		,,	,,	,,
2611 ,, Sage, C.		,,	,,	,,
2717 Trooper Lacey, W.		,,	,,	,,
2931 ,, Leslie, F.		,,	,,	,,
2879 ,, Thornton, W.		,,	,,	,,
2832 A./Corp. Beal, A.		,,	,,	,, (Died.)
3044 Trooper Winter, G.		,,	,,	,,
2805 ,, Gerber, J.		,,	,,	,,
2784 ,, Beavis, S.		,,	,,	,,
2853 ,, Banner, A.		,,	,,	,,
2640 ,, Watkins, T.		,,	,,	,,
2600 ,, Pryke, W.		,,	,,	,,
2939 ,, Smith, W. R.		,,	,,	,,
2678 ,, Boyle		,,	,,	,,
2839 ,, Stribling, R.		,,	,,	,,

WAR DIARY OF

2273	Trooper	Breakspear, H.	1st Life Guards	Wounded	13/5/15
2789	,,	Sweetnam, J.	,,	,,	,,
2934	,,	Warwick, F.	,,	,,	,,
2902	,,	Brown, S.	,,	,,	,,
2955	,,	Jenkins, A. A.	,,	,,	,,
3067	,,	Frend, G. W.	,,	,,	,,
2783	,,	Lewis, H.	,,	,,	,,
2868	,,	Southam, J.	,,	,,	,,
2412	,,	Bint, W.	,,	,,	,,
2777	,,	Moore, H.	,,	,,	,,
2971	,,	Dabson, W.	,,	,,	,,
2244	,,	Burton, V.	,,	,,	,, (Died.)
1966	C. of H.	Bonnard, H.	,,	,,	,,
2474	Corporal	George, W.	,,	,,	,,
3064	Trooper	Garlick R.	,,	,,	,,
2724	,,	Ashby, T.	,,	,,	,,
4144	L. Cpl.	Snelling	3rd D. Guards	,,	,,
4657	Private	Bennett, N.	11th Hussars	,,	,,
8161	,,	Askill, R.	1st Life Guards	,,	,,
5217	,,	Elliott, H.	6th Dragoons	,,	,,
4025	,,	Milner, R.	3rd D. Guards	,,	,,
2507	,,	Thornton, A.	6th Dragoons	,,	,,
8607	,,	Paton, G.	2nd Dragoons	,,	,,
5318	,,	Ollier, G. W.	6th Dragoons	,,	,,
5016	,,	Attwood, A.	2nd Dragoons	,,	,,
8357	,,	Ruff, H.	6th D. Guards	,,	,,
8319	,,	Lorimer, J.	2nd Dragoons	,,	,,
2516	,,	Crier	6th Dragoons	,,	,,
6655	,,	Hodge, F.	7th D. Guards	,,	,,
6211	,,	Payne, B. W.	1st D. Guards	,,	,,
5717	Corporal	Parker, T.	6th Dragoons	,,	,,
1040	Private	Miller C.	7th D. Guards	,,	,,
698	,,	Irwin, B.	6th Dragoons	,,	,,
3137	,,	Burgess, W.	11th Hussars	,,	,,
5985	,,	Witcher, H.	1st D. Guards	,,	,,
3895	,,	Simpson, W.	,,	,,	,,
4629	,,	Ward, D. G.	5th D. Guards	Missing	,,
2489	Trooper	Johnston, J.	1st Life Guards	,,	,,
5986	Private	Rowledge	1st D. Guards	,,	,,
6300	Trooper	Cowley, G.	,,	,,	,,
2932	,,	Williamson, P.	,,	,,	,,
3111	,,	Hannan, O. S.	,,	,,	,,
8939	Private	Lewis, H.	6th D. Guards	,,	,,
2855	Trooper	Sillence, A.	1st Life Guards	,,	,, Unofficially reported killed. 13/5/15.
2786	,,	Hall	,,	,,	Unofficially reported wounded.
5494	Private	Weston, P.	2nd D. Guards	,,	,, ,,
5638	Corporal	Vann, W.	1st D. Guards	,,	,, ,,

Killed	..	25
Wounded	..	59
Missing	..	11

Potijze—**May 14, 2.30 A.M.**—Regiment moved into General Headquarters' line, where it remained all day, Brigade forming Divisional Reserve. Captain J. C. G. LEIGH and 1 other rank joined B Echelon from Base.

At 9 p.m. 2nd Cavalry Division relieved 3rd Cavalry Division, and regiment retired to huts at VLAMERTINGHE.

B.M.41.
To 1st Life Guards.

Following Divisional Order G.727 received, begins: " 3rd Cavalry Division will be relieved to-night by the 5th Cavalry Brigade. The relieving troops of the 5th Cavalry Brigade will be at Cross Roads at POTIJZE at 9.0 p.m. when they will be met by a Staff Officer of 6th Cavalry Brigade, together with their own guides who will hand over the line of fire trenches to the relieving party. As soon as the 5th Cavalry Brigade move off from the Cross Roads, details of 7th and 8th Cavalry Brigades now in General Headquarters line will move off from the trenches by the road running through (I. 4.c.) to POTIJZE and thence return to their huts W. of YPRES under arrangements to be made by General Officer Commanding 8th Cavalry Brigade. Troops relieved from the firing line will proceed to their huts W. of YPRES under Brigade arrangements.

1st LIFE GUARDS

"If troops of other Brigades or Divisions are met when debouching into the main POTIJZE—YPRES road precedence will be given to troops already marching on that road.

"Three half-limbers per regiment will be formed upwith tail of column at POTIJZE Cross Roads ready to move off S.W. by 8.15 p.m. in the following order, 7th Cavalry Brigade, 8th Cavalry Brigade. Parties will be ready at that hour to load up limbers which will move off to billets at 8.30 p.m." (Ends.) Regiments will be careful to make up arms, equipment, tools, etc., as far as possible to the number brought up, from those at present lying in vicinity of General Headquarters' line, and will load up these, as above, on their limbers. Boxes of ammunition will be left.

Details of 8th and 7th Cavalry Brigades will move off from the trenches in the following order—Royal Horse Guards, Essex Yeomanry, N. Somerset Yeomanry, Leicester Yeomanry, 1st Life Guards, 2nd Life Guards. As they are relieved Regiments will march independently, at slight intervals, to their huts W. of YPRES, moving from the trenches by the route laid down in Divisional Order G. 727.

From 7th Cavalry Brigade.

B.M.42.

To 1st Life Guards.

Following received from 3rd Cavalry Division (begins): "Following messages to be communicated to the troops. First one begins: 'Express my appreciation of the magnificent spirit shown by the troops to-day and the way they have stuck to their position.—General Plumer.' (Ends.) Second message begins: 'General Joffre has expressed to the Lieut.-General Commanding 5th Corps his admiration and congratulations on the gallant stand they have made.'" (Ends.)

From 7th Cavalry Brigade.   D. P. T.

Vlamertinghe—May 15, 16, 17.—Passed in huts without incident, eight other ranks joined B Echelon from Base during these three days.

B.M.43.

To 2nd Life Guards.

For the present the 7th Cavalry Brigade with a Battalion of Infantry will form the 1st mobile reserve, ready to march, ½-hour after receipt of order at 7th Cavalry Brigade Headquarters. All units of 7th Cavalry Brigade will turn out all men who are properly equipped and will only take a proportion of officers suitable for number of men taken—*c.g.* not more than four officers per hundred men. Starting Point—railway crossing. Order of march—2nd Life Guards, 1st Life Guards, Leicestershire Yeomanry.

From 7th Cavalry Brigade.   D. P. T.

Vlamertinghe—May 18.—Brigade furnished digging party of 200 men, 75 from regiment under 2nd Lieut. L. PAYNE-GALLWEY, to dig in General Headquarters' line.

With reference to action on May 13th, it should be noted that Machine-gun in advance trenches was lost, but one in *point d'appui* was recovered after dark by 4 men of machine-gun section.

Vlamertinghe—May 19.—Passed without incident.

Vlamertinghe—May 20.—Quiet day, digging party under Captain E. HELY went up to YPRES in evening.

To 1st and 2nd Life Guards, Leicestershire Yeomanry and 7th Cavalry Field Ambulance.

The Commanders of the 2nd Army, Cavalry Corps, and 3rd Cavalry Division have all expressed to the Brigadier their admiration of the conduct of the Brigade during the recent operations, when in order to relieve Infantry sorely tried and greatly reduced in numbers, it was called upon at short notice to occupy incomplete trenches and then, within three hours, to withstand a violent bombardment and attack.

In communicating this appreciation the Brigadier desires to add his congratulations and thanks to all ranks in the Brigade for their most gallant conduct in a very trying situation.

Deeply though he deplores the losses sustained, he feels that the gratitude of the whole Brigade is due to the Commander and personnel of the 7th Cavalry Field Ambulance, also to the Medical Officers and their assistants with units, for their untiring energy and wholehearted devotion to duty, which saved so many lives.

D. P. TOLLEMACHE, Captain,
20/5/15.   Brigade-Major 7th Cavalry Brigade.

WAR DIARY OF

Ebblinghem—May 21.—Regiment returned to billets by motor bus starting at 9 p.m.

Following officers joined in billets during absence of regiment :—

>Capt. J. C. C. LEIGH (exchanging with Major Sir F. H. W. CARDEN).
>Capt. Hon. E. S. WYNDHAM, D.S.O. (To command A Squadron *vice* Capt. G. E. M. MUNDY suffering from shock.)
>Capt. P. W. FOSTER.
>Capt. Earl of CALEDON.
>Lieut. C. D. LEYLAND.
>Lieut. Sir P. BROCKLEHURST.
>Lieut. H. MATHEY.

Ebblinghem—May 22-27.—Passed without incident beyond the arrival of a reinforcement of 129 other ranks on 23rd.

Ebblinghem—May 28.—Regiment moved to billets at CAMPAGNE, EBBLINGHEM area having been allotted to 2nd Cavalry Division.

>A.K.93.
>
>*May 28th.*—The Brigade as verbally detailed will proceed by motor buses to VLAMERTINGHE to-morrow in relief of the 5th Cavalry Brigade holding the ramparts of YPRES South of the MENIN GATE. Motor buses will be at the following places for regiments to embark at 1 p.m.
>
>>Headquarters .. one bus at WARDRECQUES.
>>1st Life Guards .. 14 buses at Cross Roads south of P. in CAMPAGNE.
>>2nd ,,   ,, .. 12 ,, just west of WARDRECQUES Station.
>>Leicestershire Yeo. 6 ,, at WITTES.
>
>As soon as loaded, buses will proceed to join column at WARDRECQUES Station.
>
>The column is due to arrive at VLAMERTINGHE at 6.30 p.m., and troops will probably not start from there on foot to YPRES until 8.15 p.m. On arrival at YPRES ramparts, Regiments will take over dug-outs from Regiments of 5th Cavalry Brigade as under.
>
>*On left.*—1st Life Guards. 2 squadrons from Scots Greys and 1 squadron from left-hand squadron 12th Lancers.
>
>*Centre.*—Leicestershire Yeomanry from two right squadrons 12th Lancers.
>
>*Right.*—2nd Life Guards from 20th Hussars.
>
>The machine gun detachments of 1st and 2nd Life Guards will on arrival at VLAMERTINGHE get into touch with the 3rd Dragoon Guards and will accompany that Regiment when it starts for the trenches. Machine-guns and ammunition being taken on pack from VLAMERTINGHE. A Echelon wagons as verbally communicated and machine-gun pack-horses will proceed to VLAMERTINGHE under the Brigade transport officer and will bivouac west of the town as last time. Officers commanding will insure that this transport is at WARDRECQUES Station at 8.45 a.m. to-morrow ready to march.
>
>Supplies for the 30th will be brought up to the ramparts in A Echelon vehicles.
>
>Whilst in the ramparts medical arrangements will be regimental. Ambulances will be sent up to the ramparts after dark each night to evacuate sick or wounded.
>
>E. W. S. BALFOUR, Staff Captain,
>7th Cavalry Brigade.
>
>7.15 p.m.

Campagne—May 29.—Regiment embussed and proceeded to VLAMERTINGHE as per A.K.93.

A and D Squadrons took over from Royal Scots Greys in ramparts, B Squadron from 12th Lancers.

>A.K.96.
>
>*May 29th.*—While occupying dug-outs in the ramparts the following precautions must be observed :—
>
>1. Men are not to be allowed to wander about on the top of the ramparts during daylight and should remain in their dug-outs.

1st LIFE GUARDS

   2. Cooking must be done in the dug-outs so far as possible. Fires lighted outside are apt to cause shelling. In fact every precaution must be taken to avoid attracting attention.

   3. Each regiment is to maintain a patrol permanently in the trenches at the top of the ramparts to give notice of the approach of poisonous gas. At night these patrols are to be under officers, one from each regiment.

   4. Returns of strength-officers and other ranks, actually with units in the ramparts are to be rendered by 9 a.m. to-morrow.

   5. Casualty returns for previous 24 hours to be rendered to Brigade Headquarters daily at 6 p.m.

D. P. TOLLEMACHE, Captain,
Brigade-Major 7th Cavalry Brigade

The Machine-gun Section under Captain Earl of CALEDON was attached to the Squadron of 3rd Dragoon Guards commanded by Major P. MASON. They occupied trenches designed for all round defence immediately S. of MENIN road at HOOGE.

Ypres—May 30 and 31.—Nothing to report, except that on 31st trenches occupied by 3rd Dragoon Guards were very heavily shelled, several feeble infantry attacks by the enemy were repulsed. Captain Earl of CALEDON was wounded, and Machine-gun Section lost 1 man killed and 5 wounded.

Ypres—June 1.—A quiet day. At 8.30 p.m. a digging party of 200 men under Capt. J. J. ASTOR went up and dug behind front line S. of HOOGE. Machine-gun Section rejoined, having been relieved by infantry.

Ypres—June 2.—Again quiet. Digging party under Capt. P. W. FOSTER went forward as per B.M.70.

   B.M.70.
   1st Life Guards.
   Leicestershire Yeomanry.
   Essex Yeomanry.

   Working parties will be found to-night as under :—

1st Life Guards	Officers 2		Men 70
Leicestershire Yeomanry	,, 1		,, 60
Essex Yeomanry	,, 2 (including 1 Captain)		,, 70
Total	,, 5		,, 200

   The Captain Essex Yeomanry will command the whole party. The party will not leave the Sailly Port before 8.45 p.m. and will be at the Ecole at 9 p.m. where the officer in charge will report to the O.C. 3rd Field Squadron R.E.

   Tools.—The Leicestershire Yeomanry will bring the 4 picks and 16 shovels, and the Essex Yeomanry the 10 shovels which they possess, and will have handed over to them by 1st Life Guards at 8.30 p.m. at the Sailly Port the following tools—

   Leicestershire Yeomanry   10 picks.   30 shovels } as far as it is possible to make up
   Essex Yeomanry   ..   15   ,,   45   ,,   } these numbers.

   Rifle and 1 Bandolier to be carried.

D. P. TOLLEMACHE, Captain,
Brigade-Major.

Ypres—June 3.—No incident during day. At 8.30 p.m. regiment moved to ZOUAVE WOOD, 800 yds. S.W. of HOOGE, in accordance with G.20 J.

   G.20 J.
   To G.O.C. 7th Cavalry Brigade.
   An attack is being made to-night on certain tactical points N. of HOOGE.

WAR DIARY OF

The 1st Life Guards will move up at once to the Dumping-ground where they will come under the orders of Brig.-General Campbell and will be met by a guide. No greatcoats, only rifle, bayonet and 2 bandoliers, respirators and iron rations required. Acknowledge.
From 3rd Cav. Div., 7 p.m.

At 12.30 a.m. left ZOUAVE WOOD to return to ramparts, services not having been required.

Wires exchanged between regiment and His Majesty on occasion of his birthday.

Wires—

"Officers, N.C.O.'s and men of Your Majesty's First Regiment of Life Guards now serving abroad wish to convey their congratulations with their humble and devoted loyalty on the occasion of Your Majesty's birthday.

STANLEY, Commanding 1st Life Guards."

Following for Officer commanding the 1st Life Guards 7th Cavalry Brigade, Expeditionary Force—" Please convey to all ranks my best thanks for their congratulations on my Birthday and my appreciation of the gallant services they have rendered during the past months.—GEORGE R.I."

Ypres—June 4 and 5.—All quiet. At 4.30 p.m. regiments marched from ramparts, on relief by H.A.C., and proceeded to VLAMERTINGHE, where the night was passed.

S.C.54.   5.6.15.

To O.C. 1st Life Guards.

1. The Brigade will embus to-morrow at 12.30 p.m. on the VLAMERTINGHE-POPERINGHE road about 1 mile west of VLAMERTINGHE and will return to billets.

2. Busses 1-6 Leicestershire Yeomanry.
   Bus 7 Brigade Headquarters.
   Busses 8-21 1st Life Guards.
   Busses 22-33 2nd Life Guards.

3. Echelon A. will return to billets under the Brigade Transport Officer as soon as it has filled up at the huts.

4. Leave applications should reach the Staff Captain by 3 p.m. to-morrow with the names and destinations, the home address and the dates of absence.

E. W. S. BALFOUR, Captain,
Staff Captain 7th Cavalry Brigade.

Vlamertinghe—June 6.—At 12.30 p.m. regiment embussed in accordance with S.C.54, and returned to CAMPAGNE.

Full casualties for week—

CASUALTY LIST.

Capt.	Earl of Caledon.	Wounded.	1/6/15.		
2822	Trooper Redley, E.	Killed	,,		
2890	,, Payne, T.	Wounded	,,		
2864	,, Powell, F.	,,	,,		
2984	,, Bangs, A.	,,	,,		
2265	,, Birch .	,,	,,		
2730	,, Harding, P.	,, shock	,,		
5446	A/Corpl. Bodel, E.	Killed	2/6/15.	(6th Dragoons.)	
3258	Trooper Dingle, G.	Wounded.	,,		
3453	,, Kynaston, J.	,,	,,		
3042	,, Woolley, F.	,,	,,		
2509	Private McSherry, J.	,,	,,	(6th Dragoons.)	
8326	,, McFayden, J.	,,	,,	(2nd Dragoons.)	
2811	Trooper Reeves, W.	,, (gas)	,,		

SPECIAL ORDER
by
MAJOR-GENERAL C. J. BRIGGS, C.B.,
Commanding 3rd Cavalry Division.

HEADQUARTERS,
7th June, 1915.

The Second Army Commander has requested the G.O.C. to convey to all ranks his gratitude for the good work they have recently carried out to the East of YPRES.

1st LIFE GUARDS

The Army Commander recognises the difficult task which was allotted to the troops of the Division, especially on the left of the line, and has expressed his appreciation of the gallant manner in which the position was held and maintained under most difficult and trying circumstances.

The G.O.C. wishes to add his own appreciation and congratulations to those of the Army Commander for the good work performed by all ranks of the Division.

C. C. NEWNHAN, Lieut.-Colonel,
A.A. & Q.M.G., 3rd Cavalry Division.

SPECIAL ORDER
by
MAJOR-GENERAL C. J. BRIGGS, C.B.
Commanding 3rd Cavalry Division.

HEADQUARTERS,
12th June, 1915.

The 5th Corps Commander has requested the G.O.C. Cavalry Corps to convey to all ranks of the 3rd Cavalry Division, an expression of the hearty thanks and sincere admiration of the 5th Corps for the good work recently carried out by the 3rd Cavalry Division at YPRES.

J. C. BROWNE, Major,
D.A.A. and Q.M.G., 3rd Cavalry Division.

The following officers went up to YPRES with regiment on above occasion:—

Major A. M. Pirie, D.S.O., Capt. Hon. E. S. Wyndham, D.S.O., Capt. J. J. Astor, Capt. R. H. Stubber, Capt. Hon. E. H. Wyndham, Capt. Earl of Caledon, Capt. P. W. Foster, Capt. Sir P. Brocklehurst, Lieut. C. D. Leyland, Lieut. H. Matthey, 2nd Lieut. Boswall-Preston, 2nd Lieut. C. Trafford, Surg.-Lieut. E. D. Anderson.

Owing to Lieut.-Col. STANLEY being on leave in England, Major PIRIE took command.

Campagne—June 7-15.—Passed without incident in billets.

On June 13th Capt. P. W. FOSTER unfortunately was kicked by a horse and broke his leg.

On June 12th 2nd Lieut. J. C. MURRAY and 10 other ranks joined from the Base.

To O.C.

From 6 a.m. to-morrow all units of the Brigade will maintain such degree of readiness that they can reach the places of concentration in two hours' time from receipt of orders at their Headquarters.

Places of concentration are as follows (the ST. OMER-AIRE road being referred to as the main road):—

A. For mounted troops of all three regiments, in the field on the western side of the main road, just west of W. in WITTES, where a Staff Officer will meet them.
B. The Machine-Gun Sections of all three regiments will accompany their units to their places of concentration, and will there be brigaded.
C. "K" Battery, R.H.A. on the main road facing south—head at T road N.W. of W. in WITTES.
D. "A" Echelon, on main road facing south in rear of "K" Battery.
E. 7th Cavalry Field Ambulance, on main road in rear of "A" Echelon.
F. "B" Echelon (less "B" Echelon Leicestershire Yeomanry) on main road facing south head at RACQUINGHEM.

"B" Echelon, Leicestershire Yeomanry, will form up in column of route on the main road in WITTES facing south.

(Signed) D. P. TOLLEMACHE, Captain,
Brigade-Major, 7th Cavalry Brigade.

15th June, 1915.

WAR DIARY OF

Campagne—June 16.—Regiment stood to in accordance with Brigade Order.

Campagne—June 17.—Passed without incident except that degree of readiness was extended from 2 hours to 3½ hours.

Campagne—June 18.—The Field Marshal Commanding-in-Chief inspected the Brigade, and complimented them on the services they had rendered during the recent fighting at YPRES.

Campagne—June 19-22.—Nothing to report.

Campagne—June 23.—Following officer and other ranks of the regiment appeared in the list of those mentioned in Despatches published in the *London Gazette*, June 22nd :—

> Surg.-Lieut. E. D. ANDERSON.
> 2570 Corpl. A. FABRAY.
> 2297 Corpl. C. STANGHAN.
> 2442 Trooper S. J. CLEMENTS.
> 8319 Private J. LORIMER (2nd Dns.)

Campagne—June 24-28.—Nothing to report.

Campagne—June 29.—Regiment furnished a digging party of 45 other ranks which proceeded by motor-bus to NEUVE EGLISE to dig a reserve line of trenches in that neighbourhood. Major A. M. PIRIE, D.S.O., accompanied them to command the three parties furnished by the Brigade.

Campagne—June 30.—Nothing to report.

Campagne—July 1.—Nothing to report.

Campagne—July 2.—Four complete turn-outs of limbered waggons arrived for the Machine-gun Section on augmentation of establishment. In addition to the eight drivers accompanying above, a draft of 7 other ranks joined from Base.

Campagne—July 3-5.—Nothing to report, except that on 4th, 2nd Lieuts. H. A. BROWN and O. S. PORTAL joined.

Campagne—July 6.—The digging-party under Major A. M. PIRIE, D.S.O., was relieved by one under Lieut. G. H. BOSWALL-PRESTON.

Campagne—July 7-10.—Nothing to report.

Campagne—July 11.—A further digging-party of 45 men was furnished under 2nd Lieut. G. T. TRAFFORD for work in 8th Division area. They proceeded by motor-bus to SAILLY STATION.

Campagne—July 12.—2nd Lieut. H. A. BROWN relieved Lieut. G. H. BOSWALL-PRESTON in command of the digging-party at NEUVE EGLISE.

1st LIFE GUARDS

Campagne—July 13.—Lieut. G. H. BOSWALL-PRESTON proceeded to England in accordance with War Office instructions for employment under Munitions Office.

Quiestede—July 15.—Regiment moved to billets at QUIESTEDE, A Squadron at COUBRONNE. This move was dictated by the necessity of clearing the line of the ST. OMER-AIRE and ST. OMER-HAZEBROUCK roads for 3rd Army on its way to the front.

Major L. E. BARRY, who had been attached to the regiment supernumerary since December, 1914, as Officer Commanding A Echelon transport of the Brigade, left to take over the duties of A.P.M. 3rd Cavalry Division.

Quiestede—July 16-20.—Nothing to report.

Quiestede—July 20.—The digging-party at NEUVE EGLISE was relieved by another party of same strength under Capt. J. C. G. LEIGH.

A party consisting of 2nd Lieut. G. G. BARKER and 57 other ranks proceeded by motor-bus to ELVERDINGHE to put the village in a state of defence. (Two days later Capt. E. HELY also went up to act as Adjutant to the O.C. 3rd Cav. Div. digging-party here.)

For the second time the Chief Engineer 3rd Army Corps sent a very complimentary letter to G.O.C. 3rd Cavalry Division on the work carried out by digging-parties found by Division at NEUVE EGLISE.

Quiestede—July 21-24.—Nothing to report except the return of NEUVE EGLISE party under Capt. LEIGH except 1 N.C.O. and 10 men who were left to complete work.

Quiestede—July 26.—The regiment strength—9 officers and 282 other ranks (including 2 officers and 57 other ranks already there)—proceeded by motor-bus to ELVERDINGHE. A working-party of 900 men was required there, and this number was completed by the Royal Horse Guards under Major H. E. BRASSEY and 3rd Dragoon Guards under Lieut.-Col. A. BURT. Lieut.-Col. Hon. A. F. STANLEY, D.S.O., was in command of the whole party, and administrative commandant of all troops in ELVERDINGHE. Regiments bivouacked in the château grounds, and dug for 6 hours daily. A few shells occasionally fell in the village, but no casualties occurred. All ranks took considerable interest in the work, which continued till August 5th, when 3rd Cavalry Division party was relieved by 9th Cavalry Brigade.

Quiestede—July 31.—Lieut. J. H. KIRKWOOD and 9 other ranks joined from base.

WAR DIARY OF

Names of Officers, First Life Guards, who have been awarded Decorations for service in the Field.

Lieut-Colonel	Hon. A. F. Stanley, D.S.O.	London Gazette, 1st December, 1914.
Captain	Hon. E. S. Wyndham, D.S.O.	London Gazette, 1st December, 1914.
Captain	Hardy, L. H.	Awarded the Military Cross, London Gazette, 16th Feb., 1915.
Lieutenant	Smith, A. L.	Awarded the Military Cross, London Gazette.

Roll of N.C.O.'s and Men, First Life Guards, awarded the Distinguished Conduct Medal.

2048	C. of H.	Attenborough, G.	For conspicuous gallantry and devotion to duty on the 13th May, 1915, near YPRES, when he remained in shell holes under a heavy fire during a retirement, and ultimately advanced with the 10th Hussars in a counter attack.
2798	,,	Fleming, H.	On 6th November showed great coolness and gallantry during advance, and was wounded within 10 yards of the enemy's trenches.
2569	,,	Rose, A.	For conspicuous gallantry on 20th November in re-occupying his trench after being twice blown out by shell fire. Was subsequently killed.
3043	,,	Baillie, J.	Behaved with great coolness on 6th November by collecting men in the firing line and advancing with them in the attack. Helped a wounded man back to safety and returned to firing line.
2399	A/Corp.	Beach, E.	For gallantry in carrying messages under fire from Squadron to Headquarters, and for subsequent good work whilst temporarily attached to the 2nd Life Guards.
1653	Trooper	Lewis, R.	For gallantry on 6th November. Always volunteering, he carried several messages under fire.

Roll of Officers, First Life Guards, Killed, Died, Wounded or Missing.

KILLED.	DIED OF WOUNDS.	MISSING.
Major Lord John Cavendish, D.S.O.	Colonel Cook, M.V.O.	Captain Lord Hugh Grosvenor.
Lieut. Hon. R. Wyndham.		,, E. D. F. Kelly.
2nd Lieutenant St. George.		Lieutenant J. C. Close Brooks
Lieutenant Hulton Harrup.		,, A. L. Smith.
Lieutenant Sir R. Levinge, Bart.		,, Hon. G. Ward.

WOUNDED.

Viscount Althorp	Lieutenant.		Fitzroy, Hon. A.	Captain.
Astor, J. J.	Captain.		Hardy, L. H.	Captain.
Brassey, E. H.	Lieut-Colonel.		Leigh, J. C. G.	Captain.
Brocklehurst, Sir P.	Lieutenant (Captain Derby Yeomanry).		Leyland, C.	Captain.
			*Sutton, Sir R.	Captain.
Bostock	2nd Lieutenant.		Seton Kerr	Lieutenant.
Butler, G.	Captain.	The Marquis of Tweeddale	Captain.
Earl of Caledon	Captain.		Wyndham, Hon. E. S., D.S.O.	Captain.
Cowie, R. M.	Surgeon-Major.		Woolley	Lieutenant.
Denison, Hon. H.	Lieutenant.			

* Twice wounded.

Roll of Officers, First Life Guards, serving with Divisional Squadron on August 4th, 1915.

Major	B. D'A. Corbet.		Lieutenant	F. L. Reeves.
Lieutenant	Lord Somers.		2nd Lieutenant	H. A. Pelly.
,,	A. N. Spicer.		,,	R. G. Thynne.

1ST LIFE GUARDS

Roll of Officers, First Life Guards, with the British Expeditionary Force, 1914-1915.

Lieutenant H. Aldridge.
Lieutenant Viscount Althorp. W.
Surgeon-Captain E. D. Anderson.
Captain J. J. Astor. W.
2nd Lieutenant G. G. Barker.
Lieutenant R. Bingham.
2nd Lieutenant S. C. Bostock. W.
Lieutenant-Colonel E. H. Brassey, M.V.O. W.
Lieutenant Sir P. Brocklehurst, Bart. W.
Lieutenant J. C. Close Brooks. M.
2nd Lieutenant H. A. Brown.
Captain J. G. Butler. W.
Captain Earl of Caledon. W.
Captain Sir F. Carden, Bart.
Major Lord John Cavendish, D.S.O. K.
Captain St. G. Clowes.
Colonel E. B. Cook. (Died of wounds.)
Captain B. Corbet.
Surgeon-Major R. M. Cowie. W.
Lieutenant Hon. H. Denison. W.
Captain Hon. C. C. Fellowes.
Captain Hon. A. E. Fitzroy. W.
Captain W. Foster.
2nd Lieutenant L. Payne Gallwey.
Hon. Capt. W. G. Garton.
2nd Lieutenant H. St. George. K.
Captain H. M. S. Goodliffe.
Captain Lord Hugh Grosvenor. M.
Lieutenant J. G. Hallswell.
Captain L. H. Hardy. W.
Lieutenant Hulton Hurrup. K.
Captain T. Hely.
2nd Lieutenant E. R. Hoare.
Captain E. D. F. Kelly. M.
Lieutenant J. H. Kirkwood.

Captain J. C. Leigh. W.
Lieutenant Sir R. Levinge, Bart. K.
Lieutenant C. Leyland. W.
Lieutenant H. W. Matthey.
Captain J. Miller Mundy.
2nd Lieutenant J. C. Murray.
Captain Viscount Newry and Mourne.
2nd Lieut. T. Nottidge.
2nd Lieutenant H. A. Pelly.
Major A. Pirie, D.S.O.
Captain W. R. Portal.
2nd Lieutenant O. S. Portal.
Lieutenant G. Preston.
Lieutenant F. L. Reeves.
Lieutenant T. H. Robson.
Lieutenant H. M. Seton Karr. W.
Lieutenant A. L. Smith. K.
Lieutenant Lord Somers.
Lieutenant A. N. Spicer.
Lieutenant-Colonel A. F. Stanley, D.S.O.
Captain R. Hamilton Stubber.
Captain Sir R. Sutton, Bart. W.
2nd Lieutenant R. G. Thynne.
Lieutenant-Colonel H. H. Duke of Teck, G.C.B., G.C.V.O., C.M.G.
2nd Lieutenant G. T. Trafford.
Captain The Marquis of Tweeddale. W.
Lieutenant Hon. G. Ward. M.
2nd Lieutenant C. Waterhouse.
Lieutenant J. Woolley. W.
Captain Hon. E. H. Wyndham.
Captain Hon. E. S. Wyndham, D.S.O. W.
Lieutenant Hon. R. Wyndham. K.
Hon. Captain C. Yeatman.

K—Killed.   M—Missing.   W—Wounded.

Roll of Officers, Reserve Regiment, First Life Guards.

Lieutenant-Colonel Sir G. L. Holford, K.C.V.O., C.I.E.
Major Lord Penrhyn.
Major E. W. Clowes, D.S.O.
Captain C. S. Schrieber.

Captain Lord Leconfield.
Captain Duke of Abercorn.
Riding-Master Hon. Lieut. L. Plumb.
Qr.-Master Hon. Major Wragg.

WAR DIARY OF

FIRST LIFE GUARDS.

Roll of N.C.O.'s and Men Killed in Action, or Died from Wounds received in Action.

No.	Rank.	Name.
2770	Trooper	Black, J.
2880	C. of H.	Leggett, W.
2719	A/Corp.	Moore, F. W.
2663	Trooper	Peverill, R.
2847	,,	Brown, S. H.
2693	A/Corp.	Adams, C.
2920	Trooper	Dennes, V.
2965	,,	Lewry, E.
2682	,,	Rogers, F. S.
2870	,,	Scothern, J.
2411	,,	Levy, W. G.
2429	,,	Bishop, W.
2686	,,	Sollars, S.
2061	A/S.C.M.	Holmes, C.
2876	Trooper	Wood, J.
2569	C. of H.	Rose, A.
2871	Tptr.	Brown, S.
2959	Trooper	Spoor, C. R.
2922	,,	Helliwell, T. H.
1972	C. of H.	Bruce, P.
2828	Trooper	Ford, A. J.
6266	,,	Robinson, J.
2427	C. of H.	McFeeley, G.
2947	A/Corp.	Clay, W.

No.	Rank.	Name.
2905	Trooper	Westley, R. W.
3054	,,	Abrahams, M. G.
2809	A/Corp.	Kimpton, E.
2929	Trooper	Roberts, W.
2818	,,	Pearce, C.
2817	,,	Golding, C. G.
2802	Corporal	Castle, E. P.
2666	Trooper	Flaxman, W.
2859	,,	Russell, C.
2714	,,	Arnold, A.
2326	C. of H.	Coates, J.
3103	Trooper	Moores, J.
3080	,,	Pye, O.
2916	Corporal	Gibson, A. J.
2955	Trooper	Jenkins, A. A.
2287	,,	Ruscoe, A.
2889	A/Corp.	Rowe, D. E.
2832	,,	Beale, A.
2741	Trooper	Whittaker, S.
3088	C. of H.	Storey, E. H.
2882	Trooper	Redley, H.
2855	,,	Sillence, A.
2244	,,	Burton, V.
2900	,,	Hickling, H.

Roll of Wounded N.C.O.'s and Men, First Life Guards.

No.	Rank.	Name.
2724	Trooper	Ashby, T.
2971	,,	Adams, F. J.
2853	,,	Banner, A.
2883	Corporal	Bowler, E.
2984	Trooper	Bangs, A.
2902	,,	Brown, S.
1966	C. of H.	Bonnard, A.
2832	A/Corp.	Beal, A.
2265	Trooper	Birch F.
2784	,,	Beavis, S.
2412	,,	Bint, J.
2273	,,	Breakspear, H.
2483	,,	Brown, W.
2954	Trooper	Banks, H.
2797	,,	Baxter, W.
2848	,,	Bowler, A. L.
2747	,,	Bomford, R.
2762	,,	Bussey, H.
2891	,,	Bray, H.
2887	,,	Coomer, C.
2830	,,	Cocksworth, C.
2636	Cpl. S.S.	Colbran, G.
3774	A/Corp.	Corner, F. G.
2863	,,	Chapman, A.
3235	,,	Dingle, G.
2975	,,	Dabson, W.
2715	Trooper	Ellis, E.
2798	C. of H.	Fleming, J. H.
3067	Trooper	Frend, G. H.
2805	,,	Gerber, J.
2907	,,	Gregory, B. A.
3064	,,	Garlick, R.

No.	Rank.	Name.
2474	A/Corp.	George, W.
2785	Trooper	Gray, S.
2648	,,	Gates, F. C.
2730	,,	Harding, P.
2438	,,	Henley, E.
2558	C. of H.	Hart, H. J.
2913	Trooper	Hunt, A.
2683	,,	Impleton, J.
2562	,,	Juniper, A.
2955	,,	Jenkins, A. A.
2516	F.C. of H.	Johns, H. A.
3452	Trooper	Kynaston, J.
2931	,,	Leslie, F.
2745	,,	Luckman, W.
2793	,,	Lewis, H. J.
2718	,,	Lacey, W.
2899	A/Corp.	Marriage, W.
2777	Tptr.	Moore, H.
2608	Trooper	Marsh, C.
2462	C. of H.	Oram, E. H.
2818	Trooper	Pearce, C. H.
2864	,,	Powell, F.
2600	,,	Pryke, W.
2890	,,	Payne, T. G.
2216	,,	Pearson, F.
2426	,,	Rees, C. H.
2670	,,	Rhodes, W.
2908	,,	Roberts, W. A.
2158	S.C.M.R.	R.Ratcliffe, J.
2611	Corporal	Sage, C.
2789	Trooper	Sweetnam, J.
2936	,,	Smith, W. R.

1st LIFE GUARDS

No.	Rank.	Name.	No.	Rank.	Name.
2839	Trooper	Stribbling, W.	2464	Cpl. S.S.	Webb, P.
2874	,,	Smith, F.	2934	Trooper	Warwick, F.
2443	,,	Scott, N.	2589	C. of H.	Wilcox, P. G.
2879	,,	Thornton, F.	3042	Trooper	Woolley, F.
2746	,,	Thompson, C. E.	3004	,,	Winter, J.
3096	,,	Thompson, E.	2640	,,	Watkins, T.
2443	C. of H.	Tapsell, H.	2052	C. of H.	Webb, W. S.
2616	,,	Tobin, F.	2575	,,	Wright, C.

Roll of Wounded who afterwards Died.

No.	Rank.	Name.	No.	Rank.	Name.
2244	Trooper	Burton, V.	2719	A/Corp.	Moore, F.
2429	,,	Bishop, W.	2663	Trooper	Peverell, R.
1927	C. of H.	Bruce, P.	3008	C. of H.	Storey, E. H.
2828	Trooper	Ford, A. J.	2870	Trooper	Scothern, J.
2411	,,	Levy, W. G.	2905	,,	Westley, R. W.

FIRST LIFE GUARDS.

Roll of N.C.O.'s and Men reported as "Missing."

No.	Rank.	Name.	No.	Rank.	Name.
2350	C. of H.	*Dawes, H. W.	2780	Trooper	Berry, J.
2563	,,	Wise, J.	2025	,,	Fair, D. H.
2966	Trooper	Blackmore, A. J.	2739	,,	*Woodward, W.
2529	,,	Paget, F.	2447	,,	*Savage, H.
2759	,,	Proberts, J.	2952	,,	Williamson, P.
2345	,,	Streeter, H.	3111	,,	Hannan, T. S.
2979	,,	White, J. J.	2489	,,	Johnston, J.
2827	,,	*Lord, H.	2705	Corporal	Pate, T
2744	,,	*Gladman, W.			

* Reported Wounded and Missing.

FIRST LIFE GUARDS.

List of Prisoners of War interned in Germany.

No.	Rank.	Name.	Place of Internment.
2502	Corporal	Kitson, J.	Gefangenen-Lager Senne II. Via Paderborn.
2771	Trooper	Freegard, F.	
2483	,,	Brown, W.	Gefangenen-Lager, Senne I. Via Paderborn.
2895	,,	Geeves, J.	Gefangenen-Lager, Gottingen Proving of Hanover.
2518	,,	Groombridge, R.	
2570	Corporal	Fabray, F.	Kriegsgefangener, Baracke No. 4
2812	Trooper	Tubb, S.	,, ,, No. 1 — Arbeitslager, Suderzallhaus Schleswig, Via Gustrow in Mecklenburg.
2574	,,	Law, S. G.	,, ,, No. 4
3047	,,	Clark, C.	,, ,, No. 4
2863	,,	Chapman, A.	
2694	,,	Ormston, G.	Gefangenen-Lager, Block 9 (3), Doeberitz, Deutschland.
2852	,,	Westcott, P.	
2653	,,	Lewis, R.	No. 6 Coy. Zerbst Anhalte.
2438	,,	Henley, E. G.	Gefangenen-Lager Soultan Hanover.
2753	,,	Basson, O.	

WAR DIARY OF

FIRST LIFE GUARDS.

List of N.C.O.'s and Men to join Expeditionary Force, France.

	No.	Rank.	Name.		No.	Rank.	Name.
H	1553	R.C.M.	Baker, J. H.		2647	A/C. of H.	Utton, C.
	2258	,,	Coggins, S.		2609	Corporal	Lethbridge, W.
H	1814	Q.C.M.	Meakin, P. T.	P	2753	,,	Basson, O.
H	2028	,,	Kemp, C.	D	2809	,,	Kimpton, E.
	2687	F.Q.C.	Mackenzie, J. K.		2611	,,	Sage, C.
	2200	F.S.C.	Rose, A.		2652	A/C. of H.	Sykes, J.
	2051	S.C.M.	Brown, W.		2688	,,	Lindsdell, G.
	1983	Q.C.M.	Duffield, F.		2673	,,	Boylin, G.
	1802	S.C.M.	Rudd, G.		2535	Sad. Corporal	Barry, D.
	1929	,,	Sensier, R.		2728	Corp. S.S.	Dear, C.
H	2080	,,	Phillips, W.		2451	Corporal	Brown, J.
	2032	,,	Paul, E.		2399	A/Corporal	Beach, E.
	1819	S.Q.C.	Harrison, W.	H	2691	,,	Cowdery, E.
	1817	,,	Jones, E.	H	2474	,,	George, W.
	1893	,,	Brown, A.		2851	A/C. of H.	Hobbs, G.
	1885	,,	Kieley, A.		2787	A/Corporal	Burrows, W.
	1894	S.C.M.	Gulliver, J.	D	1972	C. of H.	Bruce, P.
H	3061	S.Q.C.	Gregory, E.	D	2569	,,	Rose, A.
D	2061	A/S.C.M.	Holmes, C.	D	2719	A/Corporal	Moore, F.
H	2158	S.C.M.R.R.	Ratcliffe, J.	H	2676	C. of H.	James, J.
	2136	O.R.S.C.M.	Fisher, B.		2831	A/Corporal	Martin, L.
	2048	C. of H.	Attenborough, G.		2496	,,	Morrison, J.
	2499	C. of H.	Putman, F.		2297	,,	Stanghem, C.
	2315	,,	Horseman, A.		2606	A/Corporal	Whitehorn, N.
H	1966	,,	Bonnard, H.		2729	,,	Young, S.
D	2326	,,	Coates, J.	P	2570	Corporal	Fabray, A.
H	2367	,,	Williams, A.		2598	Corporal S.S.	Hayes, W.
H	2407	,,	Hughes, F.		2812	A/Corp.S.T.M.	Lister, W.
	2458	,,	Wright, A.		2667	A/Corporal	Bell, J.
	2225	S.Q.C.	Dawes, C.		2837	,,	Blackwell, H.
H	2589	C. of H.	Wilcox, P.	M	2705	,,	Pate, T.
	2612	,,	Bentley, W.		2473	,,	Gosden, S.
	2541	,,	Butson, W.		2792	,,	MacDonald, A.
H	2513	,,	Haywood, G.		3038	A/C. of H.	Duke, H.
	2029	,,	Ayers, J.		3234	,,	deWilton, C.
H	3043	A/C. of H.	Bailey, J.	H	3048	A/Corporal	Swann, H.
M	2350	C. of H.	Dawes, H.		2762	,,	Bussey, H.
	2798	A/C. of H.	Fleming, H.		3113	,,	Martin, J.
H	2517	,,	Gotheridge, C.		3096	A/C. of H.	Thompson, E.
	2484	C. of H.	Hyland, R.		2983	Corporal S. S.	Sherwood, F.
	3026	,,	Hogg, W.		3102	A/Corporal	Rudge, C.
D	2880	,,	Leggett, W.		3083	,,	Rainbird, F.
H	2462	,,	Oram, E.		2247	C. of H	Calrow, J.
	2757	,,	Shepherd, W.		2005	F. C. of H.	Lambert, R.
H	2432	,,	Tapsell, H.		2608	A/Corporal	Marsh, C.
M	2565	,,	Wise, J.		3490	,,	Grimsdell, E.
	2375	,,	Wright, C.		2558	C. of H.	Hart, H.
H	2050	,,	Webb, S.		2932	A/Corporal	Harknett, A.
	2622	,,	Yarnall,		2205	C. of H.	Hancock, A.
H	2749	A/C. of H.	Channon, A.	D	2427	,,	McFeeley, G.
	2829	,,	Lloyd, R.	D	2593	A/Corporal	Adams, C.
	2229	F.S.C.	Hammon, W.		3175	,,	Jones, O.
	2141	,,	Pettit, S.	D	2802	Corporal	Castle, E.
	2578	S.S.C.	Knight, J.	H	2641	C. of H.	Watkins, F.
	2552	F. C. of H.	McFeeley, E.	H	2803	Corporal	Bowler, A.
	2033	Sad. S.C.	Dibbell, E.	D	2889	A/Corporal	Rowe, D.
H	2516	F. C. of H.	Johns, H. A.	D	2714	Trooper	Arnold, A.
	2440	C. of H.	Randell, R. J.		2962	,,	Amey, C.
D	3088	C. of H.	Storey, C.	H	2761	,,	Abbott, J.
	3058	C.S.S.	Huggett, W.		3069	,,	Ainslie, C.
	2866	Corporal	Clarke, C.	H	3087	,,	Allaway, H.
	2471	,,	Hodgson, G.	D	3054	,,	Abraham, M.
	2597	,,	Smith, W.		2834	Tptr.	Allen, G.
M	2549	,,	Neighbour, T		2971	Trooper	Adams, F.
P	2502	,,	Kitson, J.	H	1936	,,	Adlam, J.

H—Home.   M—Missing.   D—Deceased.   P—Prisoner.

68

1st LIFE GUARDS

No.	Rank.	Name.	No.	Rank.	Name.
2660	Trooper	Allchin, N.	3706	Trooper	Back, C.
2985	,,	Andrews, A.	3302	,,	Bracewell, H.
H 2724	,,	Ashby, T.	3510	,,	Beattie, D.
2782	,,	Askey, F.	3386	,,	Brompton, H.
3016	,,	Absolm, H.	3590	,,	Berry, A.
3116	,,	Aubrey, W.	2713	,,	Carrington, G.
3538	,,	Agg, A.	2941	,,	Conroy, T.
3481	,,	Alexander, T.	H 2742	,,	Cartwright, T.
H 2678	,,	Boyle, A.	P 2863	,,	Chapman, A.
2801	,,	Belsey, N.	2953	,,	Crocker, T.
2126	,,	Blackmar, F.	2533	Tptr.	Clarke, W.
2101	,,	Benson, G.	H 2781	Trooper	Champion, W.
2810	,,	Best, C.	2845	,,	Chapman, W.
H 2891	,,	Bray, H.	2912	,,	Collyer, A.
2707	,,	Blackburn, F.	2512	,,	Collins, G.
2651	,,	Briggs, C. R.	3057	,,	Codman, B.
D 2847	,,	Brown, S.	2088	,,	Champion, G.
2797	,,	Baxter.	H 1887	,,	Coomer, C.
H 2899	Corporal	Marriage, W.	H 2416	,,	Chesterton, C.
2814	A/Corporal	Barber, R.	2505	,,	Cousins, A.
2875	,,	Proctor, D.	2487	,,	Cunning, W.
D 2947	,,	Clay, D.	2442	,,	Clemments, S.
D 2832	Corporal	Beal, A.	2320	,,	Curchin, A.
H 2848	,,	Bowler, E.	2964	,,	Cook, W.
2632	,,	Bowl, E.	H 2774	,,	Corner, F.
M 2780	,,	Berry, J.	P 3047	,,	Clarke, Z.
2658	,,	Bailey, T.	2318	,,	Cooper, J.
2716	Trooper	Bliss, J.	3073	,,	Clarke, W. V.
2927	Corporal	Barlow, G	3052	,,	Crayston, T. E.
H 2902	,,	Brown, S.	3257	,,	Catchpole, S.
2365	,,	Blythe, N.	3215	,,	Chenery, H.
H 2784	,,	Beavis. S.	3120	,,	Crockett, S.
2967	,,	Barnes, J.	3524	,,	Clark, V.
H 2853	,,	Banner, A.	3568	,,	Chambers, J.
2453	,,	Batchelor, E.	2830	,,	Cocksworth, C.
D 2871	Tptr.	Browne, S.	3145	,,	Clough, S.
D 2429	Trooper	Bishop, W.	3275	,,	Carpenter, R.
H 2984	,,	Bangs, A.	3206	,,	Cockett, H.
2727	,,	Brown, E.	3065	,,	Conner, J.
2553	,,	Burge, A.	3235	,,	Cooper, A.
2441	,,	Burge, P.	3244	,,	Carr, H.
2747	,,	Bomford, R.	3345	,,	Colvin, T.
2319	,,	Brown, A.	3027	,,	Cross, R.
H 2954	,,	Banks, A.	3759	Sadd.	Chivers, J.
D 2244	,,	Burton, V.	3415	Trooper	Cave, G.
P 2483	,,	Brown, W.	3502	,,	Collett, H.
H 2265	,,	Birch, F.	2397	,,	Candy, C.
H 2412	,,	Bint, W.	2972	,,	Collins, A.
2239	,,	Barnard, J.	3397	,,	Coles, F.
M 2966	,,	Blackmore, A.	3444	,,	Clarke, F.
3085	,,	Beckham, W.	3315	,,	Carter, W.
D 2770	,,	Black, J.	3086	,,	Cox, H.
3135	,,	Bibby, A.	3569	,,	Champ, H.
H 3002	,,	Berterelli, A.	3645	,, S.S.	Cadman, W.
3237	,,	Bower, E.	3487	,,	Cross, J.
3128	,,	Butler, J.	3411	,,	Craiggs, A.
3212	,,	Bradshaw, F.	3148	,, S.S.	Cornford, W.
3230	,,	Barker, F.	2791	,,	Dunford, F.
3272	,,	Brann, F.	H 2734	,,	Douglas, J.
3282	,,	Barclay, F.	2942	,,	Doyle, H.
2365	,,	Blythe.	2791	,,	Dunford, F.
3305	,,	Burnett, E.	2366	,,	Donaldson, R.
3218	,,	Baker, W.	2679	,,	Done, R. A.
3194	,,	Baglow, H.	H 2975	,,	Dadson, W.
3267	,,	Ballantyne, T.	3024	,,	Dodson, S.
3133	,,	Back, L.	3266	,,	Dunlop, W.
3122	,,	Blake, H.	H 3252	,,	Dingle, G.
3476	,,	Bessant, F.	3300	,,	Duffield, J.
3311	,,	Baird, E.	3382	,,	Dickenson, C.
3365	,,	Bird, E.	3186	,,	Doherty, F.
3360	,,	Bosworth, H.	3343	,,	Deardon, T.
3242	,,	Bennison, T.	3417	,,	Dunny, P.

H—Home.   M—Missing.   D—Deceased.   P—Prisoner.

WAR DIARY OF

	No.	Rank.	Name.		No.	Rank.	Name.
	3396	Trooper	Douglas, R.		3463	Trooper	Grange, E.
D	2920	,,	Dennes, V.		3453	,,	Gosling, C.
	3402	,,	Dipper, J.		3117	,,	Greaves, R.
	3437	,,	Dryden, J.		2806	,,	Hall, E.
	3439	,,	Dunn, G.	H	2949	,,	Houlding, J.
	3370	,,	De Renzey, T.		2634	,,	Huggins, H.
	3109	,,	Down, F.		2755	,,	Holt, H.
	3139	,,	Dales, C.		2867	,,	House, F.
	3134	,,	Dorien, W.		2767	,,	Humby, H.
	2926	,,	Ellison, A.		2883	,,	Hopper, T.
	2519	,,	Easby, C.		2743	,,	Hopkins, G.
	3190	,,	Everett, A.		2935	,,	Hammond, J.
	3344	,,	Evershed, G.	H	2479	,,	Hume, J.
	2715	,,	Ellis.		2617	,,	Haydon, H.
	3406	,,	English, R.	H	2298	,,	Hussey, R.
D	2828	,,	Ford, A.		2400	,,	Hall, S.
D	2666	,,	Flaxman, W.	P	2438	,,	Henley, E.
	2940	,,	Faithorn, A.	H	2413	,,	Hughes, S.
	2768	,,	Field, B.		2730	,,	Harding, P.
H	2436	,,	Flint, C.	H	2028	,,	Higginbottom, C.
	2599	,,	Franklin, W.	H	2148	,,	Howell, A.
	3066	,,	Frend, W.		3191	,,	Hill, S.
H	3067	,,	Frend, C.		2994	,,	Haworth, F.
	3060	,,	Finch, W.		3093	,,	Hoskins, H.
P	2771	,,	Freegard, F.		3161	,,	Hereford, T.
H	2926	,,	Finlow.		3020	,,	Heighton.
M	2025	,,	Fair, D.		3017	,,	Hewitt, C.
H	2950	,,	Freestone.		3188	,,	Holliday, H.
	2355	,,	Finn, D.	D	2922	,,	Helliwell, T.
H	2735	S.S.	Fennemore.		3001	,,	Holmes, E.
	3004	Trooper	Finnimore, H.	M	3111	,,	Hannan, H.
	3090	,,	Foster, F.		3258	,,	Haggar, F.
	3245	,,	Fisher, H.		3138	,,	Hill, A.
	2556	Tptr.	Godwin, R.		3358	,,	Haynes, G.
	2515	Trooper	Goodall, W.		3377	,,	Hunter, J.
D	2916	,,	Gibson, A.		3403	,,	Henderson, S.
M	2744	,,	Gladman, W.		3262	,,	Hartley, R.
	2819	,,	Gale, T.		3381	,,	Hills, A.
P	2985	,,	Geeves, J.		2913	,,	Hunt, F.
	2521	,,	Godfree, E.		3189	,,	Hyde, L.
	2843	,,	Glasby, H.		3371	,,	Hobday, W.
	2945	,,	Gostelow, H.		3422	,,	Humberstone, J.
D	2817	,,	Golding, C.		3786	S.S.	Hooper, F.
	2914	,,	Gallop, H.		3408	,,	Hill, S.
	2354	Farr.	Greening, S.		3425	,,	Hay, R.
H	2805	Trooper	Gorber, J.		3391	,,	Hill, L.
	2921	,,	Gathercole, G		3532	,,	Hervey, F.
H	2648	,,	Gates, F.		3404	,,	Henderson, J.
	2613	,,	Giles, C.		3441	,,	Hills, J.
P	2518	,,	Groombridge, R.		3063	,,	Hill, C.
	2733	,,	Griffin, A.		3223	,,	Havell, F.
	3010	Tptr.	Gaston, A.		3468	,,	Hammond, A.
	2486	Trooper	Gamble, C.	H	2863	,,	Impleton, J.
	2785	,,	Gray, S.		2776	,,	Jackson, H.
	2943	,,	Greest, A.		2311	,,	Jordon, A.
	2403	,,	Grace, W.		2717	,,	Jeal, F.
	3072	,,	Grayson, T.	D	2955	,,	Jenkins, A.
H	3195	,,	Greaves, A.		3048	,,	Jestico, P.
	3136	,,	Gladding, H.		2562	,,	Juniper, A.
	3179	,,	Griffin, H.		2461	,,	Jordon, A.
	3348	,,	Gordon, J.	M	2486	,,	Johnstone, J.
	3318	,,	Greenway, G.		3068	,,	Johnson, W.
	3112	,,	Goodard, D.		3028	,,	Johnston, G.
H	2423	,,	Gill, E.		3149	,,	Jones, F.
	3143	,,	Gould, R.		3551	,,	Jarvis, G.
	3229	,,	Gillespie, A.		3686	,,	Jackson, E.
	3385	,,	Gordon, K.		3176	,,	Jefferson, A.
	3127	,,	Green, E.		3274	,,	Jones, A.
	2892	,,	Goodall, F.		3316	,,	Jones, A.
	2907	,,	Gregory.		2379	,,	Johnstone, R.
	3494	,,	Grimsdell, A.		2928	,,	Kenlock, M.
	3405	,,	Greatrex, F.		3452	,,	Kynaston, J.

H—Home.   M—Missing.   D—Deceased.   P—Prisoner.

1st LIFE GUARDS

	No.	Rank.		Name.		No.	Rank		Name.
	3331	Trooper		Kemp, M.		3394	Trooper		Molsher, M.
	3281	,,		Kinnemouth, J.		3511	,,		Major, C.
	3165	,,		Kemp, E.		3380	,,		Mutgatroyd, A.
	3499	,,		King, W.		3303	,,		Mitchell, R.
	3284	,,		Kemp, C.		2990	,,		Monk, A.
	2557	,,		King, W.		3559	,,		Mold, F.
	2999	,,		Lewis, B.		3451	,,		Mills, C.
	2064	,,		Lappage, G.		2500	,,		Nesbit, E.
H	2718	,,		Lacey.		3056	,,		Nicholls, W.
H	2931	,,		Leslie, F.		3241	,,		Neale, A.
	2948	,,		Lifford, A.		3465	,,		Nugent, H.
	2745	,,		Luckman, W.		2285	,,		Newman, J.
M	2827	,,		Lord, H.		3159	,,		Newsome, E.
	2957	,,		Lynch, T.		3158	,,		Newsome, J.
	2793	,,		Lewis, H.		2704	,,		Orton, J.
	2342	,,		Lindridge, K.		2665	,,		Oakey, E.
H	3030	,,		Ladds, W.	P	2694	,,		Ormston, G.
	2956	,,		Ladd, W.		3035	,,		Olliver, H.
H	2527	,,		Lawrence, W.		3278	,,		Ogbourne, H.
	2410	,,		Look, J.		3321	,,		O'Conner, A.
	2542	,,		Lane, E.		3168	,,		Outhwaite, H.
D	2411	,,		Levy, W.		3100	,,		Parsons, C.
	2628	,,		Lovell, A.		3136	,,		Porter, W.
D	2965	,,		Lewry, E.		3105	,,		Pearce, J.
	2503	,,		Long, C.		3231	,,		Perrins, W.
P	2653	,,		Lewis, R.		3209	,,		Phillips, A.
P	2574	,,		Law, G.		3137	,,		Pressland, E.
	3202	,,		Lyons, A.		2669	,,		Price, L.
	3170	,,		Lack, H.		2813	,,		Pontin, W.
	3167	,,		Lindsay, J.	D	2663	,,		Peverell, R.
	3285	,,		Lane, E.		2626	,,		Pritchett, A.
	3295	,,		Layton, G.		2878	,,		Pilgrim, G.
	3493	,,		Large, V.	H	2600	,,		Pryke, W.
	3362	,,		Long, W.	D	3080	,,		Pye, J.
	3119	,,		Lowe, S.		3192	,,		Pritchard, A.
	3480	,,		Lewis, S.		2470	,,		Pouncett, G.
	3426	,,		Lewellyn, P.	M	2529	,,		Pagett, F.
	3464	,,		Lambourne, T.	M	2759	,,		Proberts, J.
	3563	,,		Lawrence, F.		2316	,,		Pearce, G.
	3547	,,		Lane, A.	H	2890	,,		Payne, T.
						2864	,,		Powell, F.
	2795	,,		Marshall, W.	H	2216	,,		Pearson, F.
	2894	,,		Markwick, W.		3260	,,		Pritchard, T
	2885	,,		Macey, H.		3233	,,		Pugh, J.
	2923	,,		Milton, G.		3125	,,		Page, C.
	2404	,,		Martin, L.		3261	,,		Purvis, W.
	2750	,,		Mather, J.		3277	,,		Pring, S.
	2763	,,		MacLeod, M.		3297	,,		Pitkin, W.
H	2919	,,		Macullum, J.	D	2818	,,		Pearce, C.
H	2777	Tptr.		Moore, H.		3271	,,		Pink, J.
	2710	Trooper		Moore, A.		3107	,,		Percy, H.
D	3103	,,		Moores, J.		3427	,,		Pettitt, W.
	2496	,,		Morrison, J.		3114	,,	S.S.	Pritchard, J.
	2534	,,		Morris, S.		3185	,,		Revington, J.
	3108	,,		Mawer, A.		3226	,,		Richardson, P.
	3091	,,		Mills, W.		3149	,,		Rowland, A.
	3173	,,		Moorcroft, R.		3354	,,		Redding, J.
	3089	,,		Mariner, E.		3155	,,		Rimmer, C.
	3130	,,		Moralee, D.		3033	,,		Ranford, W.
	3007	,,		Morris, G.		3144	,,		Ramage, J.
	3095	,,		May, H.		2501	,,		Robinson, T.
	3197	,,		Miles, A.		3075	,,		Robinson, L.
	3227	,,		Martin.		3151	,,		Raper, S.
	2997	,,		Maddocks, F.	H	2670	,,		Rhodes, W.
	3283	,,		Miller, A.	D	2929	,,		Roberts, W.
	3542	,,		Moon, H.	D	2882	,,		Redley, H.
	3543	,,		Moon, D.		2591	,,		Rogers, W.
	3330	,,		Maunder, R.		2893	,,		Roberts, A.
	3340	,,		Miller, R.	D	2859	,,		Russell, C.
	2000	,,	S S.	McCaa, J.	D	2674	,,		Raines, J.
	3320	,,		McKillop, A.		2908	,,		Roberts, W.
	3264	,,		Marshall, J.		3039	,,		Russell, B.
	3014	,,		Moody, G.		2595	,,	S.S.	Ramage, W.

H—Home.   M—Missing.   D—Deceased.   P—Prisoner.

71

WAR DIARY OF

No.	Rank.	Name.		No.	Rank.	Name.
	2548	Trooper	Rodgeway, W.	H	2425	Tptr.	Taylor, D.
	2481	,,	Roy, J.		2459	Trooper	Tenneson, L.
H	2426	,,	Rees, C.	P	2872	,,	Tubb, S.
	2607	,,	Russell, A.		2968	,,	Tomlin, W.
H	2811	,,	Reeves, W.		3050	,,	Thomas, F.
D	2287	,,	Ruscoe, A.		3118	,,	Tucker, J.
D	2682	,,	Rogers, F.		3214	,,	Thompson, P.
D	6266	,,	Robinson, J.	H	3032	,,	Taylor, H.
H	2856	,,	Rock, E.		3092	,,	Thrussell, R.
	3187	,,	Resh, A.		3208	,,	Tasker, S.
	3124	,,	Rickwood, E.		3355	,,	Tyler, L.
	3312	,,	Rutter, G.		3279	,,	Thompson, V.
	3238	,,	Rea, A.		3280	,,	Thompson, F.
	3322	,,	Robinson, G.		3319	,,	Thompson, G.
	3259	,,	Rich, H.		3286	,,	Tilbury, B.
	3342	,,	Rhoades, J.		3460	,,	Turner, C.
	3419	,,	Robertson, R.		2775	,,	Underwood, W.
	3434	,,	Robinson, C.		3104	,,	Underhill, B.
	3273	,,	Raine, W.		2604	,,	Vitler, C.
	3571	,,	Robertson, R.	H	3082	,,	Vye, G.
	3253	,,	Ranson, H.		2523	,,	Vincent, C.
	3485	,,	Ruthven, J.		3023	,,	Vigurs, J.
	3515	,,	Riley, C.	H	2662	,,	Wightman, R.
	3129	,,	Robertson, W.	D	2905	,,	Westley, R.
	1994	,,	Stevens, J.	D	2741	,,	Whittaker, S.
	2939	,,	Sparks, E.		2567	,,	Weet, C.
	2936	,,	Smith, W.	P	2852	,,	Westcott, P.
H	2839	,,	Stribbling, W.		2960	,,	Wasps, W.
	2789	,,	Sweetnam, J.		2640	,,	Watkins, F.
	2752	,,	Smith, S.		2740	,,	Weet, O. C.
D	2855	,,	Sillence, A.	H	2934	,,	Warwick, F.
	2499	,,	Sutton, H.	M	2952	,,	Williamson, P.
D	2959	,,	Spoor, H.		2886	,,	Willis, A.
H	2582	,,	Shepherd, G.		2543	,,	Wills, W.
M	2345	,,	Streeter, H.		3014	,,	Whittle, F.
M	2447	,,	Savage, H.	D	2876	,,	Wood, J.
	2576	,,	Scott, F.	M	2979	,,	White, J.
	2593	,,	Symonds, F.	M	2749	,,	Woodward, W.
D	2870	,,	Scothern, J.		2520	,,	Williams, W.
	2868	,,	Southam, J.		2946	,,	Wilkinson, W.
	2874	,,	Smith, F.		3211	,,	Wright, G.
D	2868	,,	Sollars, S.		3247	,,	Wright, F.
H	2443	,,	Scott, W.		3294	,,	Wilson, G.
	3051	,,	Shaw, J.		3324	,,	Wood, J.
	3025	,,	Saunders, W.		3042	,,	Woolley, F.
	3123	,,	Suttie, T.		3127	,,	White, J.
	2917	,,	Scott, W.		3336	,,	Walker, D.
	3332	,,	Somersgale, C.		3299	,,	Ward, G.
	3142	,,	Smith, T.		3239	,,	Wilkinson, H.
	2987	,,	Sparke, A.		3338	,,	Whitelaw, J.
	3006	,,	Singleton, A.		3325	,,	Wilson, H.
	3248	,,	Schofield, A.		3393	,,	Woodward, W
	3293	,,	Sayer, W.		3251	,,	Ward, D.
	3203	,,	Soley, E.		3416	,,	Wilson, W.
	3367	,,	Slipper, H.		3243	,,	Ward, J.
	3334	,,	Samuels, N.		3556	,,	Williams, E.
	3462	,,	Stevens, A.		3828	,,	Woodredge, A.
	3008	,,	Saunders, W.		3443	,,	Webb, E.
	3374	,,	Spowart, J.		3265	,,	Watts, C.
H	2579	,,	Strong, H.		2646	,,	Wallace, D.
H	3062	,,	O'Sullivan, J.		3684	,,	S.S. Woodcock, W.
	2877	,,	Tregaskes, W.		3132	,,	,, Warner, E.
P	2879	,,	Thornton, F.		3029	,,	Young, A.
	1832	,,	Tosh, J.		3217	,,	Young, D.
H	2746	,,	Thompson, C.		3428	,,	Yoxall, F.
	3096	,,	Thompson, E.		3040	,,	Yoemans, L.
	2616	,,	Tobin, E.		3313	,,	Zilwood.

H—Home.   M—Missing.   D—Deceased.   P—Prisoner.

1st LIFE GUARDS

DRAGOONS, ETC., ATTACHED.

FIRST LIFE GUARDS.

Roll of N.C.O.'s and Men, First Life Guards, reported Killed, or from having Died from Wounds, etc.

No.	Rank.	Name.	Regiment.	No.	Rank.	Name.	Regiment.
5420	Sergeant	Arthurs, J.	6th Dragoons.	6886	Private	Spenceley.	7th D. Guards.
5644	Corporal	Cordery, H.	,,	5972	,,	Smith, F.	1st D. Guards.
5614	Private	Brunsden, W.	,,	6252	,,	Stone, A.	,;
922	,,	Brooks, H.	3rd D. Guards.	5298	,,	Whitehead, G.	6th Dragoons.
5446	,,	Bodell, E.	6th Dragoons.	6110	,,	Hudgson, G.	2nd Dragoons.
6282	,,	Burrington, J.	1st D. Guards.	8345	,,	Lane.	3rd D. Guards.
5755	,,	Buckeridge, W.	6th Dragoons.	6548	,,	Hayes.	6th Dragoon.
6203	,,	Childs, T.	1st D. Guards.	6347	,,	Stewart.	,,
5400	,,	Corcoran, P.	6th Dragoons.	5263	,,	Slater.	3rd D. Guards.
4786	,,	Duffy, R.	5th D. Guards.	4934	,,	Harvey, W.	2nd D. Guards.
2537	,,	Dix, J.	,,	5612	,,	Meredith.	6th Dragoons.
5208	,,	Finch, T.	,,	4755	,,	Pitt.	—
6078	,,	Farmer, A.	1st D. Guards.	8604	,,	Reddington.	3rd D. Guards.
5639	,,	Greer, W.	,,	2501	,,	Williams.	6th Dragoons.
6785	,,	George, W.	2nd Dragoons.	6387	,,	Tingley.	2nd D. Guards.
5787	,,	Harvey, G.	2nd D. Guards.	5066	,,	Ramage.	5th D. Guards.
6445	,,	Hall, J.	,,	5128	,,	Sullivan.	2nd Dragoons.
2514	,,	Lawson, E.	6th Dragoons.	5466	,,	Crane.	6th Dragoons.
4964	,,	McMullen, H.	,,	5991	,,	Ingram, G.	1st D. Guards.
5759	,,	North, T.	1st D. Guards.		,,	Rathnell, A.	8th Hussars.
6108	,,	Rhoades, W.	1st D. Guards.				

Roll of Prisoners of War interned in Germany.

Dragoons attached to First Life Guards.

Corps.	No.	Rank.	Name.	Corps.	No.	Rank.	Name.
1st K.D. Gds.	4251	L/Corporal	Brock, J.	6th Dgns.	5653	Private	Tudball, G.
,, ,,	5768	Private	Hill, W.	,, ,,	2492	,,	Barneti. W.
5th D. Gds.	633	,,	Pratt, G.	,, ,,	5705	Sergeant	Jaggard, W.
,, ,,	5332	,,	Meadhurst, A.	5th D. Gds.	642	Private	Benbow, M.
1st K.D. Gds.	5546	,,	Jackson, W.	6th Dgns.	5637	,,	Downs, G.
6th Dgns.	2511	Corporal	Bowling, H.	7th D. Gds.	6576	,,	Plain, J.
,, ,,	2503	Private	Dixon, G.	1st K.D.G.	6213	,,	Lambard, J.

Roll of Wounded.

No.	Rank.	Name.	Regiment.	No.	Rank.	Name.	Regiment.
3876	Private	Hinton, G.	1st D. Guards.	5382	Private	Percy, H.	1st D. Guards.
6150	L/Cpl.	Evans, D.	,,	6152	,,	Barnes, E.	,,
6265	Private	Haggerstone, E.	,,	6372	L/Cpl.	Byron, L.	,,
6195	,,	Williams, P.	,,	5978	Private	Henry, F.	,,
6022	,,	Wilson, W.	,,	6427	,,	Cummings	2nd D. Guards
5985	,,	Witcher, R.	,,	4946	,,	Wood, A.	,,
6010	,,	Read, H. J.	,,	5986	,,	Warren, E.	,,
3896	,,	Simpson, W.	,,	5983	,,	Knott	,,
6171	,,	Sinclair	,,	5251	,,	Pocklington, C. T.	3rd D. Guards.
5384	Corporal	Smith	,,	4144	,,	Snelling, A.	,,
6211	Private	Payne, P. W.	,,	8332	,,	Marshall, J.	,,
6352	,,	Hale, E.	,,	6032	,,	Ferrie, P.	,,
6314	,,	Leslie, R.	,,	661	,,	Davenport, J.	5th D. Guards.
6125	,,	Martin, R. E.	,,	5069	,,	Hastings, W.	,,

WAR DIARY OF

No.	Rank.	Name.	Regiment.	No.	Rank.	Name.	Regiment.
4862	Private	Schofield, H.	5th D. Guards.	2174	Private	Lightfoot	1st K.D. Gds.
5148	,,	Hainsworth	,,	6203	,,	Cnilds	,,
4881	,,	Yalden, F.	,,	4179	,,	Savage	,,
457	,,	Skinner	,,	6265	,,	McDonald	,,
5204	,,	Sweetnam, W. C.	,,	5911	,,	Light	,,
5241	,,	Sears, T.	,,	6227	,,	Pegrum	,,
8357	,,	Ruff	6th D. Guards.	764	,,	Buckle	7th D. Gds.
6642	,,	Gilchrist	,,	6655	,,	Hodge	,,
6919	,,	Butler, R. J.	7th D. Guards.	5231	,,	Simpson	5th D. Gds.
8713	,,	Renton	2nd Dragoons.	5787	,,	Harvey	2nd D. Guards.
8319	,,	Lorimer, J.	,,	6095	,,	McCullen	,,
8607	,,	Paton, G.	,,	2537	,,	Dix	6th Dragoons.
5016	,,	Attwood, A.	,,	5466	,,	Crane	,,
8236	,,	MacFadyen, J.	,,	5217	,,	Elliott	,,
5406	,,	Stewart	6th Dragoons.	2507	,,	Thornton	,,
2408	,,	Boardman, E.	,,	5318	,,	Ollier	,,
2509	,,	McSherry, J.	,,	698	,,	Irwin	,,
3213	,,	Fraser, A.	,,	8627	,,	Brown	2nd Dragoons.
5736	,,	Edwards, H.	,,	8161	,,	McAskill	,,
5779	,,	Smith, R.	,,	3295	,,	Munday	3rd D. Guards.
5289	,,	Vernon, F. J.	,,	2921	,,	Goodsell	,,
5716	L/Cpl.	Parker, T.	,,	4755	,,	Pitt	,, (Died.)
5454	Corpl.	Roantree, J.	,,				
5675	Private	Bass, F.	,,	4025	,,	Milner	,,
5447	,,	Maunsell, S.	,,	6314	,,	Leslie	1st R. Dragoons
2516	,,	Crier, H.	,,	6159	,,	Burrows	7th D. Guards. (Died.)
5803	,,	Courtney, A.	,,				
5832	,,	Cotton, F. J.	,,	3137	,,	Burgess	13th Hussars.
2513	,,	Higgins, E.	,,	5208	,,	Finch	6th Dragoons. (Died.)
5508	,,	Brown	,,				
4657	,,	Bennett, A.	11th Hussars.	2494	,,	Stacey	,,
4339	,,	Fenton, W.	4th R.C. Regt.	8394	,,	Vassie	2nd Dragoons.
5823	,,	Mitchell	2nd R.C. Regt.	5347	,,	Stewart	6th Dragoons. (Died.)
5759	,,	North	1st K.D. Gds. (Died.)	976	,,	Russell	1st K.D. Gds.
2750	,,	Pye	,,				
5986	,,	Rowledge	,, (Missing.)				

Roll of Missing.

No.	Rank.	Name.	Regiment.	No.	Rank.	Name.	Regiment.
5358	Sergeant	Colclough, H.	6th Dragoons.	5913	Private	Maidment, E.	5th D. Guards.
5821	,,	Fraser, E.	3rd D. Guards.	4686	,,	Marsh, G.	6th Dragoons.
5852	Corporal	Middleton	,,	4985	,,	Miller, W.	,,
1715	Private	Barwell, H.	,,	4507	,,	Morley, J.	,,
5324	,,	Buckett	5th D. Guards.	5421	,,	Naismeth, T.	6th D. Guards.
4424	,,	Bow, W.	6th Dragoons.	5415	,,	Ordway, J.	3rd D. Guards.
42	,,	Burnett, F.	1st ,,	5682	,,	Phillips, E.	6th ,,
8267	,,	Buffham, W.	,,	5584	,,	Phillips, P.	6th Dragoons.
653	,,	Bolton, W.	5th D. Guards.	6360	,,	Pickett, G.	,,
5573	,,	Black, J.	6th Dragoons.	6031	,,	Pike, J.	1st D. Guards.
6249	,,	Broom, T.	1st D. Guards.	6318	,,	Rich, A.	,,
6300	,,	Cowley, G.	,,	6014	,,	Rose, S.	,,
6175	,,	Crutchley, J.	,,	5986	,,	Rowledge, E.	,,
6196	,,	Cunningham, C.	,,	4712	,,	Richards, F.	1st Dragoons.
5409	,,	Campbell, H.	6th ,,	958	,,	Richardson, A.	,,
5838	,,	Cootes, H.	6th Dragoons.	5005	,,	Randall, J.	5th D. Guards.
5507	,,	Dykes, W.	,,	5235	,,	Smart, J.	3rd D. Guards.
4946	,,	Davis, A.	,,	5381	,,	Skelly, S.	6th Dragoons.
5838	,,	Etchells, E.	,,	5919	,,	Smith, H. J.	1st D. Guards.
5211	,,	Gray, A.	5th D. Guards.	5963	,,	Simpson	,,
2520	,,	Green, C.	1st D. Guards.	288	,,	Turner, H.	,,
5851	,,	Gordon, J.	1st Dragoons.	5305	,,	Taylor, A.	,,
5223	,,	Hopkins, E.	5th D. Guards.	6675	,,	Woolward, E.	7th D. Guards.
2510	,,	Hamilton, J.	6th Dragoons.	2968	,,	Hall, J.	2nd R.R. of Cav.
8231	,,	King, T.	1st Dragoons.	5684	,,	Anderson	6th Dragoons.
5426	,,	Keogh, R.	6th Dragoons.	6324	,,	Boddie	1st D. Guards.
5385	,,	Kirkpatrick	1st D. Guards.	4438	,,	Simms	,,
6225	,,	Line, W.	,,	4629	,,	Ward	5th D. Guards.
5962	,,	Lush, W.	,,	5494	,,	Weston, P.	2nd D. Guards.
5342	,,	McDermott, H.	,,				

1st LIFE GUARDS

DRAGOONS, ETC., ATTACHED.

FIRST LIFE GUARDS.

Nominal Roll of N.C.O.'s and Men, First Life Guards, from Ludgershall.

	No.	Rank.	Name.	Regiment.		No.	Rank.	Name.	Regiment.
D	5420	Sergeant	Arthurs, J.	6th Dragoons.	H	4657	Private	Bennett, A.	11th Hussars.
	6129	,,	Betteridge.	1st K. D. Gds.		5592	,,	Berryman, F.	13th ,,
	6777	,,	Brooks, G.	7th D. Guards.	H	23522	,,	Bordicott, T.	11th ,,
	5937	,,	Castle, H.	1st K. D. Gds.	H	5372	,,	Byron, L. G.	1st K. D. Gds.
M	5358	,,	Colclough, H.	6th Dragoons.		1000	,,	Browning, A.	7th D. Guards.
M	5821	,,	Fraser, E.	3rd D. Guards.		5363	,,	Bell, H.	1st ,,
H	4127	Sad. Sergt.	Harrison.	1st K. G. Gds.		4902	,,	Barker, W.	,,
	6002	Sergeant	King, A.	,,		6257	,,	Barrow, H.	,,
H	5454	,,	Roantree, W.	6th Dragoons.	M	1715	,,	Barwell, H.	3rd ,,
P	4251	Corporal	Brock, J.	1st K. D. Gds.		4375	,,	Bean, M.	3rd Hussars.
	5873	,,	Boyles, A.	1st Dragoons.		4765	,,	Burley, E.	6th Dragoons.
P	2511	,,	Bowling, H.	6th ,,		4926	,,	Ballard, F.	4th D. Guards.
D	5644	,,	Cordery, H.	,,		5384	,,	Brinscombe, S.	,,
H	5739	,,	Deas, H.	,,		642	,,	Benbow, W.	5th ,,
	3213	,,	Fraser, A.	,,	M	5324	,,	Buckett.	
	5808	,,	Gibson, J.	,,	H	6919	,,	Butler, R.	7th ,,
	4309	,,	Gurr, H.	5th D. Guards.		5321	,,	Bates, F.	6th Dragoons.
	4601	,,	Giles, W.	1st ,,	H	5505	,,	Brown, W.	,,
D	6856	,,	Hopkins, G.	7th ,,	D	5614	,,	Brunsden, W.	,,
P	5705	,,	Jaggard, C.	6th Dragoons.	M	4424	,,	Bow, W.	,,
M	5852	,,	Middleton, W.	3rd D. Guards.	M	42	,,	Burnett, F.	1st ,,
	6136	,,	Olliver, W.	1st K. D. Gds.	H	8438	,,	Burnett, H.	,,
	5716	,,	Parker, T.	6th Dragoons.	M	8267	,,	Buffham, W.	,,
	6010	,,	Head, H.	1st K. D. Gds.	M	653	,,	Bolton, W.	5th D. Guards.
	5624	,,	Roe, E.	3rd D. Gds.		5788	,,	Burton, G.	6th Dragoons.
	6247	,,	Stammers, L.	1st D. Guards.	D	922	,,	Brooks, H.	3rd D. Guards.
H	5384	,,	Smith, J.	,,	M	5573	,,	Black, J.	6th Dragoons.
	5692	,,	Smith, J. W.	6th D. Guards.		6376	,,	Burnham, J.	1st D. Guards.
	5744	,,	Walker, W.	6th Dragoons.	M	6249	,,	Broom, T.	,,
	5826	Sad. Corp.	Andrews, L.	1st D. Guards.	D	5446	,,	Bodell, E.	6th Dragoons.
	5697	S.S.	Gallagher, J.	6th Dragoons.	D	6282	,,	Burrington, J.	1st D. Guards.
H	5955	,,	Bone, E.	1st D. Guards.		2550	,,	Bartlett, H.	6th Dragoons.
	1008	,,	Chamberlain, C.	7th ,,	D	5755	,,	Buckeridge, W.	,,
	6602	Saddler	Cullen, H.	6th Dragoons.		4607	,,	Brewer, W.	,,
	5673	S.S.	Ford, A.	1st D. Guards.		5675	,,	Bass, F.	,,
H	5571	,,	Garbett, G.	6th Dragoons.		2492	,,	Barnett, W.	,,
	5422	,,	McClean, A.	6th D. Guards.		5800	,,	Betts	,,
	6902	Saddler	Palmer, F.	7th ,,	H	2408	,,	Boardman, W.	,,
	5638	S.S.	Taylor, T.	6th Dragoons.	H	6799	,,	Blaber, G.	7th D. Guards.
	2598	,,	Webb.	,,		5306	,,	Collins, T.	6th Dragoons.
	5128	Trumpeter	Sullivan, W.	2nd ,,	M	6300	,,	Cowley, G.	1st D. Guards.
	6798	Private	Amor, T.	7th D. Guards.		2978	,,	Cooper, O.	,,
	5269	,,	Ashfield, G.	11th Hussars.		5583	,,	Creedy, T.	,,
H	5016	,,	Attwood, A.	2nd Dragoons.		4763	,,	Cramp, W.	,,
H	3282	,,	Abbott, J.	13th Hussars.		6081	,,	Coombs, T.	,,
	5234	,,	Austen, J.	4th D. Guards.				(To 12th Res. Cav. Reg.)	
	8385	,,	Attby, A.	11th Hussars.	H	5408	Private	Carter, T.	11th Hussars.
	5806	,,	Appleyard, W.	6th Dragoons.		5119	,,	Cox, A.	,,
H	5692	,,	Ashley, J.	,,	D	6203	,,	Childs, T.	1st D. Guards.
	5684	,,	Andrews.	,,		6502	,,	Cox, C.	,,
H	5756	,,	Arthurs, J.	,,		5641	,,	Churchill, R.	6th Dragoons.
	3137	,,	Burgess, W.	13th Hussars.		482	,,	Connelly, T.	6th D. Guards.
H	5880	,,	Betteridge, S.	11th ,,	M	6175	,,	Crutchley, J.	1st ,,
	5215	,,	Baldey, A.	5th D. Guards.	M	6196	,,	Cunningham, C.	,,
H	6158	,,	Bridges, H.	1st ,,	M	5409	,,	Campbell, H.	6th ,,
	764	,,	Buckle, A.	7th ,,		5438	,,	Campbell, B.	6th Dragoons.
H	6152	,,	Barnes, E.	1st K. D. Gds.		5332	,,	Cookson, G.	,,
	6353	,,	Berry, T.	,,	M	5838	,,	Cootes, H.	,,
	6338	,,	Bishop, E.	,,	H	2616	,,	Crier, H.	,,
	2841	,,	Brown, J.	2nd Dragoons.		2504	,,	Carris, W.	,,
	6307	,,	Burroughs, W.	5th D. Guards.	H	6427	,,	Cummings, J.	2nd D. Guards.
H	2447	,,	Brent, A.	3rd ,,	H	5803	,,	Courtney, J.	6th Dragoons.

H—Home.   M—Missing.   D—Deceased.   P—Prisoner.

WAR DIARY OF

No.	Rank.	Name.	Regiment.	No.	Rank.	Name.	Regiment.
6034	Private	Clarkes, W.	2nd D. Guards.	5677	Private	Hopper, W.	6th Dragoons.
D 5400	,,	Corcoran, P.	6th Dragoons.	6048	,,	Ireland, W.	1st D. Guards.
H 5832	,,	Cotton, F.	,,	2758	,,	Irvine, E.	7th ,,
5765	,,	Duff, C.	2nd ,,	694	,,	Irvine, B.	6th Dragoons.
H 4661	,,	Davenport, F.	5th D. Guards.	5426	,,	James, W.	1st D. Guards.
5493	,,	Doran, J.	6th Dragoons.	6241	,,	Jones, J.	,,
4459	,,	Dales, H.	,,	6079	,,	Johnson, H.	,,
D 4786	,,	Duffy, R.	5th D. Guards.	H 5157	,,	Joyce, A.	5th ,,
P 2503	,,	Dixon, G.	6th Dragoons.	5620	,,	Jones, A.	6th Dragoons.
M 5507	,,	Dykes, W.	,,	5724	,,	Jones, J.	3rd D. Guards.
M 4946	,,	Davis, A.	,,	H 533	,,	Kay, J.	2nd Dragoons.
5600	,,	Divine, C.	,,	5121	,,	Kelly, T.	,,
4234	,,	Dalton, J.	1st D. Guards.	H 5983	,,	Knott, W.	2nd D. Guards.
6134	,,	Drinkwater, J.	,,	M 8231	,,	King, T.	1st Dragoons.
D 2537	,,	Dix, J.	6th Dragoons.	M 5426	,,	Keogh, R.	6th ,,
2495	,,	Daly, T.	,,	5745	,,	Knott, H.	,,
P 5637	,,	Downs, G.	,,	M 5385	,,	Kirkpatrick.	1st D. Guards.
5435	,,	Dowds, J.	,,	6427	,,	Keane, P.	,,
H 6150	,,	Evans, D.	1st D. Guards.	5726	,,	Keefe, W.	,,
6958	,,	Elliott, G.	,,	5841	,,	King, T.	,,
H 5736	,,	Edwards, H.	6th Dragoons.	5993	,,	Lowe, J.	,,
M 5838	,,	Etchells, E.	,,	P 6213	,,	Lambard, J.	,,
D 5208	,,	Finch, T.	,,	M 6225	,,	Line, W.	,,
D 6078	,,	Farmer, A.	1st D. Guards.	5245	,,	Lebentz, H.	6th Dragoons.
6506	,,	Faid, J.	6th Dragoons.	H 6314	,,	Leslie, R.	1st D. Guards.
6198	,,	Fitzgerald, F.	1st D. Guards.	5375	,,	Lidster, F.	6th Dragoons.
6343	,,	Finch, A.	,,	2174	,,	Lightfoot, J.	1st D. Guards.
1225	,,	Ford, J.	,,	D 2514	,,	Lawson, E.	6th Dragoons.
6032	,,	Ferry, G.	3rd ,,	5562	,,	Leighton, J.	,,
5804	,,	Frost, J.	1st ,,	H 6255	,,	Legge, B.	1st D. Guards.
140	,,	Ferries, J.	6th ,,	M 5962	,,	Lush, W.	,,
H 298	,,	Fairbairn, J.	6th Dragoons.	6688	,,	Love, B.	7th ,,
8479	,,	Francis, D.	2nd ,,	5911	,,	Light, T.	1st ,,
H 5235	,,	Gibbs, T.	5th D. Guards.	6076	,,	Lawton, G.	,,
D 5639	,,	Greer, W.	1st D. Guards.	H 8319	,,	Lorimer, J.	2nd Dragoons.
D 6785	,,	George, W.	2nd Dragoons.	5912	,,	Morris, F.	1st D. Guards.
6225	,,	Grundy, A.	1st D. Guards.	H 6496	,,	McGuire, J.	2nd Dragoons.
5717	,,	Gayson, E.	6th Dragoons.	H 5447	,,	Maunsell, S.	6th ,,
5839	,,	Garlinge, H.	3rd D. Guards.	589	,,	Morris, J.	1st D. Guards.
H 6642	,,	Gilchrist, A.	6th ,,	1040	,,	Miller, T.	7th ,,
H 4213	,,	Green, J.	1st ,,	M 5342	,,	McDermott, H.	1st ,,
M 5211	,,	Gray, A.	5th ,,	6265	,,	McDonald.	,,
M 2520	,,	Green, C.	6th Dragoons.	H 6278	,,	Martindale, T.	,,
M 5851	,,	Gordon, J.	1st ,,	5295	,,	Munday, W.	3rd ,,
5792	,,	Gilman, G.	6th ,,	M 5913	,,	Maidment, E.	5th ,,
5468	,,	Groves, R.	6th ,,	P 5332	,,	Meadhurst, A.	6th ,,
H 5228	,,	Groves, J.	5th D. Guards.	5414	,,	Maher, H.	6th Dragoons.
5966	,,	Hinvest, J.	1st ,,	M 4686	,,	Marsh, G.	,,
H 5978	,,	Henry, F.	,,	H 2509	,,	McSherry, J.	,,
6241	,,	Hockley, A.	,,	M 4985	,,	Miller, W.	,,
6339	,,	Hibberd, A.	,,	385	,,	Moon, T.	1st ,,
8506	,,	Henderson, J.	2nd Dragoons.	323	,,	Moore, W.	,,
5332	,,	Himsworth, W.	,,	M 4507	,,	Morley, J.	6th ,,
6404	,,	Holdaway, F.	1st D. Guards.	D 4964	,,	McMullen, H.	,,
5247	,,	Haron, S.	3rd ,,	H 6125	,,	Martin, R.	1st D. Guards.
H 5922	,,	Hale, F.	1st ,,	H 5823	,,	Mitchell, J.	2nd ,,
6655	,,	Hodge, F.	7th ,,	M 5421	,,	Naismeth, T.	6th ,,
H 6205	,,	Henderson, E.	1st ,,	D 5759	,,	North, T.	1st ,,
5647	,,	Hood, W.	,,	M 5318	,,	Olliver, G.	6th Dragoons.
H 6352	,,	Hale, E.	,,	M 5415	,,	Ordway, J.	3rd D. Guards.
H 5148	,,	Hamsworth, H.	5th ,,	5417	,,	O'Toole, C.	6th Dragoons.
H 3876	,,	Hinton, G.	1st ,,	5265	,,	Pegram, G.	1st D. Guards.
D 5787	,,	Harvey, G.	2nd ,,	6159	,,	Pearson, J.	,,
5147	,,	Harrison, E.	5th ,,	6406	,,	Pike, H.	7th ,,
H 5069	,,	Hastings, W.	,,	5655	,,	Perks, F.	1st ,,
M 5223	,,	Hopkins, E.	,,	6024	,,	Pigg, T.	,,
5759	,,	Hallims, F.	6th Dragoons.	6291	,,	Price, W.	2nd ,,
P 5768	,,	Hill, W.	1st D. Guards.	H 5251	,,	Pocklington, C.	3rd ,,
M 2510	,,	Hamilton, J.	6th Dragoons.	5824	,,	Parry, M.	6th Dragoons.
H 2513	,,	Higgins, E.	,,	5327	,,	Pasklett, E.	5th D. Guards.
D 6445	,,	Hall, J.	2nd D. Guards.	M 5682	,,	Phillips, E.	6th D. Guards.
5123	,,	Hibberd, W.	5th ,,	M 5584	,,	Phillips, P.	6th Dragoons.

H—Home.   M—Missing.   D—Deceased.   P—Prisoner.

1st LIFE GUARDS.

No.	Rank.	Name.	Regiment.	No.	Rank.	Name.	Regiment.
P 633	Private	Pratt, G.	5th D. Guards.	H 4862	Private	Scholefield, J.	5th D. Guards.
H 5364	,,	Pitt, W.	6th Dragoons.	5704	,,	Skipp, G.	6th Dragoons.
M 6360	,,	Pickett, G.	,,	H 457	,,	Skinner, J.	5th D. Guards.
5382	,,	Percy, H.	1st D. Guards.	M 5919	,,	Smith, H. J.	1st ,,
H 6178	,,	Pitt, W.	6th Dragoons.	M 5963	,,	Simpson.	,,
6677	,,	Pennels, A.	7th D. Guards.	H 2502	,,	Sergeant, A.	6th Dragoons.
H 6211	,,	Payne, B.	1st ,,	8364	,,	Sutherland, J.	2nd ,,
5991	,,	Peegram, P.	,,	5575	,,	Spittle, W.	1st D. Guards.
2750	,,	Pye, J.	,,	H 4880	,,	Thompson, A.	,,
M 6031	,,	Pike, J.	,,	H 4900	,,	Thompson, E.	,,
5226	,,	Pudney, H.	6th Dragoons.	3848	,,	Turner, F.	7th ,,
H 4692	,,	Robinson, T.	5th D. Guards.	M 288	,,	Turner, H.	1st ,,
H 8713	,,	Renton, W.	2nd Dragoons.	P 5453	,,	Tudball, G.	6th Dragoons.
H 6711	,,	Reeks, G.	2nd D. Guards.	M 5305	,,	Taylor, A.	1st D. Guards.
4850	,,	Richardson.	1st ,,	5846	,,	Turnball, G.	,,
2481	,,	Roy, J.	,,	2507	,,	Thornton, A.	6th Dragoons.
5464	,,	Ryan, J.	6th Dragoons.	5507	,,	Tait, R.	6th Dragoons.
H 5398	,,	Rice, J.	,,	5784	,,	Tregilgas, J.	,,
M 6318	,,	Rich, A.	1st D. Guards.	5382	,,	Torrens, J.	,,
M 6014	,,	Rose, S.	,,	H 4884	,,	Vincent, T.	5th D. Guards.
M 5986	,,	Rowledge, E.	,,	5469	,,	Vann, W.	1st ,,
M 4712	,,	Richards, F.	1st Dragoons.	5469	,,	Veitch, J.	6th Dragoons.
M 958	,,	Richardson, A.	,,	H 5289	,,	Vernon, T.	,,
M 5005	,,	Randall, J.	5th D. Guards.	5326	,,	Wilson, H.	5th D. Guards.
5455	,,	Rowan, P.	6th Dragoons.	1041	,,	Wilcox, S.	7th ,,
D 6108	,,	Rhoades, W.	1st D. Guards.	6220	,,	Webb, T.	1st ,,
5200	,,	Smith, R.	2nd Dragoons.	H 7	,,	Wilkinson, H.	,,
4179	,,	Savage, C.	1st D. Guards.	6216	,,	Wood, J.	5th ,,
H 3896	,,	Simpson, W.	5th ,,	5752	,,	Wicks, F.	1st ,,
5659	,,	Stevens, L.	1st ,,	H 5854	,,	Williams, A.	2nd Dragoons.
4814	,,	Stanley, H.	,,	5222	,,	Wall, E.	3rd D. Guards.
D 6886	,,	Spencley.	7th ,,	H 2501	,,	Whitehouse, J.	1st ,,
4870	,,	Swain, G.	5th D. Guards.	D 5298	,,	Whitehead, G.	6th Dragoons.
4302	,,	Smith, E.	1st ,,	H 4946	,,	Wood, A.	2nd D.Guards.
6378	,,	Saunders, W.	1st D. Guards.	5628	,,	Windmill, F.	6th Dragoons.
4438	,,	Simons, G.	,,	H 8363	,,	Wright, G.	1st Dragoons.
M 5235	,,	Smart, J.	3rd ,,	5783	,,	Willbelove, E.	,,
5509	,,	Shaw, W.	6th Dragoons.	H 4889	,,	White, J.	5th D. Guards.
M 5381	,,	Skelly, S.	,,	2551	,,	Williams, R.	1st ,,
3896	,,	Simpson, W.	1st D. Guards.	6880	,,	Wagner, J.	7th ,,
10	,,	Stapley, E.	,,	5970	,,	Warren, W.	2nd ,,
H 5406	,,	Stewart, L.	6th Dragoons.	H 5986	,,	Warren, E.	,,
5241	,,	Sears, T.	5th D. Guards.	5656	,,	Wilkinson, W.	6th Dragoons.
5787	,,	Stott, H.	1st ,,	5144	,,	Wright, J.	5th D. Guards.
H 6171	,,	Sinclair.	,,	H 6022	,,	Wilson.	1st ,,
H 5204	,,	Sweetman, W.	5th ,,	5755	,,	Wedgewood, W.	6th Dragoons.
D 5972	,,	Smith, F. H.	1st ,,	M 6675	,,	Woolward. E.	7th D. Guards.
D 6253	,,	Stone, A.	,,	H 6195	,,	Williams, R.	1st ,,
H 5962	,,	Smith.	,,	6262	,,	Wright, H.	,,
5644	,,	Smith, J.	,,	H 4881	,,	Yalden, F.	,,
2944	,,	Stacey, G.	6th Dragoons.	4217	,,	Yates, F.	,,

H—Home.   M—Missing.   D—Deceased.   P—Prisoner.

Reinforcements—4th November, 1914.

No.	Rank.	Name.	Regiment.	No.	Rank.	Name.	Regiment.
5227	Private	Anderson, L.	2nd Dragoons.	8057	Private	Humphries, H.	2nd D. Guards.
5788	,,	Burton, H.	6th ,,	680	,,	Maides, W.	5th ,,
5592	,,	Child, L.	,,	7092	,,	McShane, T.	2nd Dragoons.
5517	,,	Collier, A.	1st ,,	8161	,,	McAskill, R.	,,
8471	,,	Clifford, J.	2nd ,,	8416	,,	Packer, W.	6th D. Guards.
H 4154	,,	Cornwall.	6th D. Guards.	8337	,,	Proudfoot, J.	2nd Dragoons.
5466	,,	Crane, J.	6th Dragoons.	H 8607	,,	Paton, G.	,,
5431	L. Corpl.	Dudley, G.	1st D. Guards.	H 8394	,,	Vassil, J.	,,
H 5301	Private	Finneran, T.	,,	5985	,,	Witcher, F.	1st D. Guards.
5871	,,	Fox, P.	1st Dragoons.	8179	,,	Yates, A.	6th ,,
D 6110	,,	Hudgson, G.	2nd ,,	D 8345	,,	Lane.	3rd ,,

H—Home   M—Missing.   D—Deceased.   P—Prisoner.

WAR DIARY OF

Reinforcements—8th November, 1914.

No.	Rank.	Name.	Regiment.	No.	Rank.	Name.	Regiment.
6230	Private	Brooker, W.	1st R.R. of Cav.	8567	Private	McCall.	6th D. Guards
—	—	Blackwood.	2nd ,,	8939	,,	Lewis.	,,
3751	L. Corpl.	Wakeland, A.	2nd ,,	6827	,,	Jones.	7th D. Guards.
5300	,,	Baker, G.	2nd ,,	5484	,,	Cangley.	6th Dragoons.
4210	Private	Ball, W.	2nd ,,	3842	Corporal	Goodson.	3rd D. Guards.
4024	,,	Bush, W.	6th Dragoons.	5280	,,	Chapman.	,,
7029	,,	Bush, W.	2nd R.R. of Cav.	8458	Private	Wright.	,,
5510	,,	Cradden, J.	6th Dragoons.	8703	,,	Tilbury.	,,
5472	,,	Farmer, H.	,,	281	,,	Cordwell.	,,
D 4934	,,	Harvey, W.	2nd D. Guards.	8619	,,	Mildon.	,,
M 2968	,,	Hall, J.	2nd R.R. of Cav.	D 8604	,,	Reddington.	,,
5062	,,	Lincoln, D.	,,	8154	,,	Knowles.	,,
—	,,	McNamara.	,,	8698	,,	Eggleton.	,,
H 5686	,,	Miller, B.	6th Dragoons.	H 4283	,,	Saddler.	4th D. Guards.
4290	,,	Miller, T.	2nd R.R. of Cav.	H 6901	,,	Carter.	3rd ,,
—	,,	McCullen.	,,	—	,,	Rathnell, A.	8th Hussars.
5930	,,	Moore, A.	,,	6159	,,	Burrows.	7th D. Guards.
4166	,,	Murray, A.	6th Dragoons.	H 5270	Corporal	Baker.	2nd ,,
H 4392	,,	Nicholls, F.	,,	3213	Private	Fraser.	6th Dragoons.
10335	,,	Rhodes, W.	2nd R.R. of Cav.	H 6265	,,	Haggerstone, E.	1st D. Guards.
9786	,,	Scott, J.	,,	H 5779	,,	Smith, R.	6th Dragoons.
6460	,,	Tuffin, E.	2nd D. Guards.	H 5142	,,	Wright.	,,
5052	,,	Weston, T.	,,	D 2501	,,	Williams.	,,
D 5612	,,	Meredith.	6th Dragoons.	H 5483	,,	Williams.	2nd ,,
—	,,	Lack, C.	—	H 6398	,,	Welch.	1st D. Guards.
1208	,,	Troupe.	—	H 5985	,,	Witcher.	,,
8370	,,	Fry.	6th D. Guards.	H 5964	,,	Thomas.	2nd ,,
6259	,,	Killiminster.	—	D 6387	,,	Tingley.	,,
—	,,	McDonald.	—	H 5292	,,	Waite.	6th Dragoons.
—	,,	Lock, B.	—	H 8489	,,	Robertson.	2nd ,,
D 4755	,,	Pitt.	3rd D. Guards.	H 5238	,,	Moule.	5th D. Guards.
5765	,,	Gilmartin.	3rd D. Guards.	H 8332	,,	Marshall.	3rd D. Guards.
—	,,	Gardner.	—	H 5716	Corporal	Parker.	6th Dragoons
H 8357	,,	Ruff.	6th D. Guards.	D 5066	Private	Ramage.	5th D. Guards.
3574	,,	Boshell, J.	2nd R.R. of Cav.	H 3272	,,	Stevens.	6th Dragoons.
9262	,,	Watson.	2nd D. Guards.	D 5128	,,	Sullivan.	2nd ,,
3106	,,	James.	6th Dragoons.	H 4839	,,	McPhail.	,,
3583	,,	Brockwell.	1st D. Guards.	H 8148	,,	Green.	,,
5964	,,	Thomas.	2nd ,,	H 5666	Sergeant	Burrell.	6th ,,
5217	,,	Elliott.	6th Dragoons.	H 8236	Private	McFadyen.	2nd ,,
4933	,,	Drabble.	,,	H 7092	,,	Curtis, J. G.	2nd R.R. C.R.
10134	,,	Bray.	,,	D 5466	,,	Crane.	6th Dragoons
6974	,,	Alderton, G.	11th Hussars.	H 5842	Corporal	Goodson, D.	3rd D. Guards.
5861	,,	Addison.	11th ,,	D 5991	Private	Ingram, G. T.	1st ,,
8271	,,	Corbett.	6th D. Guards.	H 6032	,,	Ferrie, G.	3rd ,,
9917	Corporal	Norman.	,,	M 5684	,,	Anderson.	6th Dragoons
8975	Private	Sheredan.	,,	M 6324	,,	Boddie.	1st D. Guards.
9180	,,	Rudge.	,,	M 4435	,,	Simms.	,,
5601	,, S.S.	Lofts.	,,	M 4629	,,	Ward.	5th D. Guards.

H—Home.   M—Missing.   D—Deceased   P—Prisoner.

1st LIFE GUARDS

Reinforcements—9th November, 1914.

No.	Rank	Name	Regiment	No.	Rank	Name	Regiment
8928	Private	Beer, W.	6th D. Guards.	D 5347	Private	Stewart.	6th Dragoons.
8389	,,	Brooks, S.	,,	6168	,,	Ferguson.	2nd ,,
6901	,,	Carter, C.	3rd ,,	9338	,,	Ingold.	6th D. Guards.
8271	,,	Corbett, R.	6th ,,	10796	Corporal	Lawrence.	,,
H 5725	,,	Cummins, R.	1st ,,	H 5377	Private	Maher.	6th Dragoons.
5223	,,	Cooper, R.	3rd ,,	H 8777	,,	Mears.	6th ,,
5811	,,	Dormer, C.	6th Dragoons.	2004	,,	McDiamid.	2nd ,,
8456	,,	Double, T.	6th D. Guards.	H 5747	,,	O'Malley.	1st D. Guards.
H 4339	,,	Fenton, P.	,,	976	,,	Russell.	,,
5235	L. Corpl.	Gibbs, T.	5th ,,	11149	,,	Smith.	,,
H 8426	Private	Greenaway, E.	6th ,,	D 5263	,,	Slater.	3rd ,,
6086	,,	Horn, W.	1st ,,	1146	,,	Towers.	6th Dragoons.
4981	,,	Huckett, W.	5th ,,	3799	,,	Barnes.	21st Lancers.
5123	,,	Hibberd, W.	,,	4024	,,	Bush, W.	6th D. Guards.
8915	,,	McLachlan, F.	,,	5689	,,	Brady, W.	6th Dragoons.
H 2692	,,	Mather, G.	,,	3583	,,	Brookwell, R.	1st D. Guards.
6227	,,	Pigrum, E.	1st ,,	3280	,,	Chapman, A.	3rd ,,
8994	,,	Sherridan, W.	6th ,,	H 5838	L. Corpl.	Downie, J.	1st R. Dragoons.
8703	,,	Tilbury, W.C.	3rd ,,	4933	Private	Drabble, H.	6th D. Guards.
5721	,,	Bradshaw, C.	6th Dragoons.	4470	,,	Long, A. W.	21st Lancers.
5838	,,	Freeman, D.	,,	8619	,,	Mildon, L.	6th D. Guards.
D 6548	,,	Heyes.	,,	H 4744	Corporal	Snelling, A.	3rd ,,
H 6891	,,	Perry, T.	7th D. Guards.	18439	Private	Scaresbrick, T.	3rd Hussars.
6991	,,	Richardson	,,	M 5494	,,	Weston, P.	2nd D. Guards.

H—Home.   M—Missing.   D—Deceased.   P—Prisoner.

FIRST LIFE GUARDS.

Permanent Staff of old First Life Guards who rejoined the Reserve Regiment.

Roll of Warrant Officers, N.C.O.'s and Men.

No.	Rank		Name	No.	Rank		Name
3121	S.C.M.		Bly, P.	3184	C. of H.		Martin, W.
3676	,,		Thompson, J.	2587	,,		Wilkinson, M.
3037	,,		Moore, C.	2495	,,		Miles, A. W.
3049	,,	I.F., & G.	Wright, W.	3172	,,		Lidstone, W.
2468	,,	(Hon.)	Scaife, A.	3225	,,		Goldsmith, A.
3061	S.Q.C.		Gregory, E.	2183	,,		Jackson, T. W.
3076	,,		Bomford, A. H.	3046	,,	Sadd.	Ford, F. S.
3287	,,		Smith, R.	3707	,,		Cripps, G. J.
3349	,,		Carter, J. W.	3718	,,	Farr.	Noller, G.
3442	S.C.M. (Hon.)		Brooks, D. G.	2386	,,		Spencer, J.
3728	S.C. Farr.		Tester, G.	3766	,,	Farr.	Leeson, A.
3757	,,		Symons, E. P.	3079	,,		Collett, R.
2494	C. of H.		Edwards, F.	3098	A/Corpl.		Hart, H. J.
3062	,,		Marshall, O. H.	2536	,,		Roberts, J.
3071	,,		McMasters, W.	2555	,,		Elder, E.
3099	,,		Elphick, J. W.				

79

A BRIEF SUMMARY

of what is being done by the First Life Guards.

On the suggestion of the ladies, we are sending parcels of food to our prisoners in Germany every fortnight.

We have heard from twenty-nine Prisoners in Germany, and Mrs. Brassey has been told of these Prisoners we have heard of, and twenty-nine parcels go out every fortnight to them.

We notify the lady of the Regiment who is looking after each prisoner, when we hear from him.

We have been having weekly lists of our N.C.O's and men who are wounded or sick in Hospital in England, these we send to the ladies who live in London, but we would be glad to send them to any one who cares to apply.

The Squadrons at home have been providing tobacco, cigarettes, etc., to their respective Squadrons abroad.

Major Wragg has been sending boots and khaki to certain prisoners who have applied direct here.

We have started a First Life Guards' Employment Society for our men who are discharged as wounded, sick or time expired, and have so far been successful in every case in finding employment.

We now have complete lists and their next of kin of all Dragoons serving with our Regiment at the Front.

In the case of pensions for widows in this Regiment, owing to pressure of work they are in many cases unprovided for between the time of the cessation of the Separation Allowance and the commencement of the Pensions; we are told this ought to improve.

There is the fund, which was organised by the Duchess of Teck and was subscribed to by Officers of the First Life Guards, past and present. This fund helps all cases of emergency or distress which occur in the 1st Life Guards.

MAP SHOWING THE PROGRESS
OF THE
COMPOSITE REGIMENT

Prepared from one lent by Major Gen! the Hon. C. Bingham, C.B.

Printed in the United Kingdom
by Lightning Source UK Ltd.
112982UKS00001BA/19-22